Ambassadors of U.S. Higher Education: Quality Credit-Bearing Programs Abroad

John Deupree and
Marjorie Peace Lenn, Editors

College Entrance Examination Board, New York

In all of its publishing activities, the College Board endeavors to present the works of authors who are well qualified to write with authority on the subject at hand and to present accurate and timely information. However, the opinions, interpretations, and conclusions of the authors are their own and do not necessarily represent those of the College Board; nothing contained herein should be assumed to represent the official position of the College Board.

Copies of this publication may be ordered from College Board Publications, Box 886, New York, NY 10101-0886. The price is $27.95.

Library of Congress Catalog Number: 96-72490

International Standard Book Number: 0-87447-569-4

Printed in the United States of America.

CONTENTS

PREFACE

The first question this book must answer is why the College Board concerns itself with issues of standards for higher education institutions offering international programming.

The answer lies in the history of the College Board's involvement with international education. The College Board is a national nonprofit membership association of schools and colleges concerned with issues of access to higher education. The Board's Office of International Education has played a long-standing role in facilitating access to U.S. higher education for prospective students from outside the United States. From these activities it became clear that students outside the United States considering investing in a U.S. education deserved clear and objective information on the potential value of their investment.

In the U.S. system of higher education, such educational value is assured through a system of quality control. When you place yourself in the shoes of a student outside the U.S. education system looking in, however, the fault lines in our quality control system are more visible than they are to someone working inside our system and looking out. Students in other countries considering a U.S. higher education are confused by institutions that have no accreditation in either the United States or the host country. They fail to understand why students attending programs offered by such institutions are sometimes able to fully transfer credits to other institutions which have clear accrediting status. They do not understand the difference between a loose linkage among professional academic colleagues and a formal, credit-bearing program offered outside of the U.S. system by a U.S. institution. Such students assume, understandably, that an institution bearing an American-like name and operating in their country must be of the same quality as one operating within the borders of the United States. Last, but not least, the more savvy among them note that standards set for educational programs offered outside the United States appear to vary depending on which U.S. regional accreditation commission has reviewed them. Together, such information leaves prospective students confused, uncertain and, in many cases, dissatisfied with their investment in a U.S.-based education.

It was while considering how to help my colleagues overseas answer these questions that I first met Marjorie Peace Lenn. At the time, Marjorie was vice president of the Council on Postsecondary Accreditation (COPA). In my world in the mainstream of international educational exchange, there had been little contact between those concerned with international student mobility and those concerned with U.S. academic quality. Marjorie was called, during the course of her tenure with COPA, to respond to a crisis of perception regarding the operation of U.S. branch campuses in Japan. This crisis had been well-documented in the groundbreaking book *Profiting from Education*,[1] published by the Institute of International Education. The serendipitous convergence of quality assurance issues and information access issues occurred because of a call for help from the U.S. Embassy in Japan, which was besieged by concerns about quality on the part of Japanese students and parents who were beginning to enroll in branch campuses in Japan in great numbers. Because my office worked closely with the United States Information Agency to ensure the quality of information available to foreign nationals on U.S. higher education, a partnership was formed that brought together quality assurance concerns with quality of access concerns. This partnership has evolved into the Center for Quality Assurance in International Education, of which Marjorie is the founder and executive director. The center is broadly concerned with issues of how academic standards can bridge political and national borders. Almost single-handedly Marjorie has created an environment in which those concerned with moving students across national borders and those concerned with the maintenance and establishment of educational standards can consider issues of mutual interest. It should be noted, however, that the center's concern with quality assurance in international education does not stop with U.S. institutions. Indeed, full academic mobility cannot be achieved until quality issues are resolved and mutually identifiable educational standards are established around the world.

---

[1] Gail S. Chambers and William K. Cummings, *Profiting from Education: Japan-United States International Educational Ventures in the 1980s* (New York: Institute of International Education, 1990).

It is because of the center's initiative, therefore, that this publication has been possible. Of course, many other individuals deserve credit for identifying and working toward resolution of issues in quality assurance as it pertains to international education. William Cummings and Gail Chambers, authors of *Profiting from Education*, articulated a number of previously unaddressed issues regarding the then-proliferation of U.S. branch campuses in Japan. Steve Crow, acting executive director of the Commission on Institutions of Higher Education of the North Central Association of Colleges and Schools, has long been an advocate of broader standards for international programs sponsored by U.S. institutions of higher education. In fact, Steve was a guiding force in the development of the standards proposed in this book. Together with staff at NAFSA: Association of International Educators, Steve also was a key force behind the *Principles of Good Practice in Overseas International Education Programs for Non-U.S. Nationals*, which served as a forerunner to the standards outlined in this book.

It is my hope that the standards presented here will serve as a pathway to consistency and quality in the manner in which U.S. institutions of higher education manifest themselves outside the geographical and educational borders of the United States. The challenge to deliver quality educational services across national borders is only beginning. The advent of new technologies is accelerating the process by which education is delivered from one country to another. There is no time to lose in building bridges to ensure that academic quality is well-defined and articulated from one education system to another. Students, who are the immediate beneficiaries of all educational services, deserve to be able to make educational choices from among institutions and programs that adhere to clear and consistent standards. Perhaps even more important, the future of civil society rides on the quality of education delivered to those students. It is for this reason that this book is dedicated to students everywhere in the world who are in search of a quality education.

John Deupree, Director,
International Education, The College Board

CHAPTER 1

Introduction: A Growing Trend in Educational Delivery

John Deupree
Director, International Education, The College Board

This book addresses a growing trend in U.S. higher education—the provision of education to new audiences in other countries. It is targeted to representatives of U.S. institutions involved in developing, operating, and/or assessing credit-bearing programs abroad. The contributors recognize, however, that this phenomenon is not uniquely American and that there are no doubt lessons within the U.S. context that can be translated broadly to the mobility of educational programs across any national borders.

The opportunity, and the perceived need, to extend U.S. educational delivery mechanisms to other education systems are natural outgrowths of the broad trend toward globalization. Educators in developing economies, accustomed to sending their students abroad for an education, now see a need to accelerate the development of higher education systems within their own political and cultural boundaries and are turning to other countries, primarily the United States, for assistance. U.S. institutions, which have traditionally received students from other countries, see the duplication of U.S.-type campuses overseas as a natural extension of their commitment to the educational process for students as well as for faculty.

Coincidental with globalization, another trend is emerging within educational circles—entrepreneurialism. Entrepreneurialism is not a new phenomenon in higher education. It has been growing ever since the first college bookstore sold its first T-shirt for a profit. Although for many years the nonprofit educational community rejected any suggestion that education might be driven by a profit motive, the education lexicon long ago stopped excluding such terms as "market" or "product." In the recent past, entrepreneurs both on and off campus have begun to see the sale of educational services as a worthy investment opportunity. Interest in establishing educational programs overseas has therefore often been accompanied by at least a perceived notion that such ventures can either pay for themselves or create revenue to be used for other institutional priorities. In some cases, this has led to the control of U.S. programs abroad at institutions falling under a fundraising scenario rather than an educational banner.

For all of these reasons, it is clear that when U.S. institutions develop and operate programs abroad, they often find themselves in new territory. The delivery of education within different cultures demands new definitions of mission and new levels of sensitivity. Those addressing questions of quality in the educational process must suddenly answer to two masters—the home institution and the host country. Although often overlooked or unforeseen, even negotiations concerning the administration of a U.S.-linked program in another country must by nature encompass matters of educational mission. In such discussions, new lines must be drawn between the financial and educational needs of the home institution and those of foreign sponsors and partners.

Inevitably, many U.S. institutions attempting to navigate in this new territory have become lost. As this book goes to press, stories are breaking about financial misunderstandings involving U.S. college administrators involved in the establishment of programs in other countries. At the same time, many U.S. institutions have launched highly successful programs abroad. What is common about the failures as well as the successes, however, is that both leave an impression on students, educators, and government officials in other countries. Fortunately or unfortunately, the impressions left may not include the names of individual institutions. U.S. international educational efforts are painted broadly and with the same brush as are the efforts of any individual college or university. When one institution stumbles, it is that much harder for others to succeed. When one succeeds, it is that much easier for others. American educational initiatives become, whether or not by intention, ambassadors for all of U.S. education, at home and abroad.

The high visibility of our educational programs abroad therefore raises the stakes of succeeding to a higher level than that of the individual institution. Two broader policy issues come into play. The first is the public policy issue of the reputation of U.S. education as a whole.

Although the United States no longer needs to curry favor around the world to ensure friends in a cold war, there remains a deep foreign policy commitment to encouraging a positive view of U.S. society and democratic ideals. The delivery of educational services is a key medium by which American ideas and ideals are conveyed to the rest of the world. When education is either poorly delivered or delivered in a context that suggests poor quality, this broader goal is diminished. Foreign service officers in a variety of countries can attest to the accelerating effects, both positive and negative, of educational initiatives undertaken by well-meaning individuals and institutions.

A second broader policy issue is more at home with the entrepreneurial flavor of many new educational initiatives—economic competitiveness. It has been said that U.S. education is the last great American industry that holds unquestioned respect throughout the world. An oft-quoted figure of about six billion dollars is used to quantify the contribution of international students to the U.S. economy. It is no secret that many other countries, notably Australia and the United Kingdom, with others in the wings, have launched efforts to reap a portion of those benefits, both economic and cultural. Any diminishing of the reputation of U.S. education therefore ultimately affects the ability of any one institution in the United States or abroad to attract students from other countries, to internationalize its campus, and to expand its educational mission.

The question of how to address the issue of economic competitiveness exposes traditional tensions between institutional autonomy and the perceived need for broader standards. Clearly, balancing individual rights and the need for regulation is at the very foundation of the democratic political process. Within U.S. higher education, the tension over standards focuses on the institution's right to autonomy versus the society's right to a quality education that will ensure that all students are capable of competing in the marketplace of the twenty-first century.

The uniquely American resolution of this tension over the years has been the concept of self-regulation. Self-regulation works when a set of mutually agreed-upon principles or standards are established. Institutions can then make their own best judgments as to how far they wish to pursue common goals. Their pursuit, or lack of pursuit, of these common goals becomes a manifestation of their mission and in

≋ *All of the contributors sincerely hope that the book will serve as a guide to those who continue to develop innovative educational initiatives in support of an educated global society.*

part determines how they fare in the market of prospective student investors.

It was with the concept of self-regulation in mind that a group of concerned international educators came together to produce this book. The book has two complementary purposes. The first purpose is to present to the higher education public a set of standards to be considered for use in the delivery of U.S. credit-bearing programs abroad. The standards were drafted by a group of experts in international education, quality assurance, and campus-based programs abroad. Among the experts were knowledgeable home-campus administrators in the United States who were particularly eager to have an externally developed set of standards to guide their own decision making. The standards are therefore offered as a chart of the still-new territory of U.S. institutionally based, credit-bearing programs abroad. They are offered without any authority or presumption on the part of the authors or organizations involved as to external enforcement. They are placed in the public record to be used as appropriate by educational institutions and quality assurance agencies in guiding their unique decision-making processes.

The second, complementary purpose of the book is to serve as a sort of primer for institutions considering the development of credit-bearing programs abroad. Without a central force guiding U.S. educational policies abroad, many institutions have reported their interest in having a source of information on issues they will face as they consider or implement programs in other countries. Toward this end the book includes chapters by expert accreditors that explain clearly U.S. institutional and program accreditation systems as they have existed to date and the international implications for those systems. Two institutional case studies—one based on the experiences of Southern Illinois University at Niigata, Japan, and the second on programs operated in Malaysia by Indiana University on behalf of a university consortium—further elucidate the pragmatic challenges of overseas program administration. Finally, staff at Southern Illinois University at Carbondale offer insights into the value of utilizing standards as program goals as negotiations within the institutional setting take place.

The chapters by Marjorie Peace Lenn and Philip J. Palin provide further background on why the U.S. effort to create and maintain standards in educational delivery abroad is being closely watched from a multinational perspective. They also point clearly to why the issues covered by this book will be paramount in meeting the challenges of the "fourth dimension"—the delivery of education through technological means.

Together, the contributors to this book wish nothing more than to assist in the delivery of quality educational programs to students throughout the world. All of the contributors sincerely hope that the book will serve as a guide to those who continue to develop innovative educational initiatives in support of an educated global society.

John Deupree is director of International Education at the College Board operating out of Washington, D.C. He is the founding chair and a member of the Council on Quality Assurance in International Education and is actively involved with numerous interassociational and multinational projects designed to increase educational access worldwide. A current initiative is the formation of a public-private partnership to ensure systematic and consistent representation of U.S. educational interests to international mobility schemes such as the UNESCO convention on the recognition of degrees and diplomas.

CHAPTER 2

Higher Education and the Global Market: The Quality Imperative

Marjorie Peace Lenn
Executive Director, Center for Quality Assurance in International Education

Saint Louis University in Madrid announces that it is accredited by the Spanish Ministry of Education, and Richmond College in London is officially recognized as a degree-granting institution in the United Kingdom. Neither case would seem remarkable except that these schools are among a large—and growing—number of accredited U.S. institutions that offer higher education abroad. The United States has exported credit-bearing programs in increasing volume, particularly in the last decade. For programs accredited in one country to seek official recognition or accreditation in other countries, however, is an emerging practice that will occur more frequently as regional and global trade agreements blur the borders of our national education systems. It is the purpose of this chapter to present the global context in which increasing exportation and international recognition of U.S. programs are taking place and to review current domestic and international policies and issues relating to the quality of the ambassadors of U.S. higher education: credit-bearing programs abroad.

The Global Context
Institutions around the world are seeking new frontiers for growth and recognition. Part of their motivation is a need for additional resources as developed countries become less capable of subsidizing higher education. But a loftier motivation lies in the rapid globalization of the marketplace and the need envisioned by the higher education community to prepare a new generation for this inevitability. In Western Europe, the phenomenon of institutions of higher education seeking multiple accreditation from the various national systems represented by their actual and prospective international students has grown rapidly in the last several months.[1] It is impossible to separate this trend from the well-funded commitment of the European Union to improve higher edu-

---

[1] Don F. Westerheijden et al., *Changing Contexts of Quality Assessment: Recent Trends in West European Higher Education* (Utrecht, The Netherlands: Uitgeverij Lemma B.V., 1994).

≋ *It is the globalization of the professions and the need to provide common professional preparation that is the fastest-moving pretense for regional and global standard setting and accreditation.*

cation opportunities as a way to assist professional mobility through better and more diverse preparation. Regional economic growth is at the heart of this change.

In 1992 the United Nations Economic, Scientific, and Cultural Organization (UNESCO) estimated the "world market" for international students as slightly in excess of 1.2 million.[2] However, this world market is measured by the number of students enrolled in educational institutions outside their country of origin as counted by receiving countries. This figure, therefore, does not take into account the unknown but perhaps even larger number of students who are receiving their education in their own country but from international sources. Whereas the United States, France, Germany, the United Kingdom, and Canada *import* the largest numbers of international students (63 percent in 1990 according to UNESCO),[3] the United States, the United Kingdom, and Australia are touted to be the primary *exporters* of higher education. The Office of the U.S. Trade Representative reports that since 1992, education has ranked fifth in U.S. cross-border sales of services, preceded by services related to travel, passenger fares, port services, and freight transportation. In 1994 the United States earned about seven billion dollars for educational services,[4] compared to one billion dollars for Australia in 1993.[5]

The growing export market in higher education, accelerated by new technologies that make distance education a primary medium, coupled with the prospect of programs seeking accreditation from receiving countries, is but indicative of a larger activity: regional and global economic growth and subsequent increased academic and professional mobility. Indeed, multiple accreditation may barely become the norm before it is supplanted by regional and eventually global accreditation, motivated by international trade agreements. These forms of quality assurance provide a system of standards and evaluation applied commonly among institutions or programs on a regional or global basis.

---

[2]United Nations Educational, Scientific, and Cultural Organization, *UNESCO Statistical Yearbook* (Paris: United Nations Educational, Scientific, and Cultural Organization, 1992).
[3]Id.
[4]Bernard Ascher, *New Trade Agreements: Implications for Education and the Professions*, QA USA, Vol. V, No. 2 (Washington, D.C.: Center for Quality Assurance in International Education, 1996).
[5]Department of Employment, Education, and Training (DEET), *Recent Trends and Current Issues in Australian Higher Education* (Canberra, Commonwealth of Australia: Department of Employment, Education, and Training, 1993).

Ambassadors of U.S. Higher Education

Although the question "what is a quality institution of higher education?" is at the heart of regional activity in the developing world, it is the globalization of the professions and the need to provide common professional preparation that is the fastest-moving pretense for regional and global standard setting and accreditation.

Examples of regional activity may be found throughout the world. In 1995 the Conference of European Rectors initiated a Europe-wide system of institutional accreditation using common standards and an international process of external review. The European Group on Academic Assessment (EGAA) was established in 1994 to address issues and processes of higher education quality in the East and West. Organized by UNESCO, EGAA and related regional organizations convene ministries of education responsible for national institutional and program accreditation and the recognition of programs taught in their countries by foreign providers. The nations of the English-speaking Caribbean have established a regional forum for quality assurance issues; the rectors of universities representing the countries of South America met in 1995 to discuss the feasibility of regional recognition and accreditation; educational ministries ringing the Indian Ocean are considering the benefits of regional cooperation in quality assurance; the African Association of Universities will focus on regional accreditation as a key theme at its 1997 annual meeting in Zambia; and there is growing interest in developing a common degree in the Asia-Pacific region.

Other recent global initiatives also underscore the rapid internationalization of higher education and the need to assess its effectiveness. The Organization for Economic Cooperation and Development (OECD) is undertaking a pilot study to evaluate the quality of the internationalizing activities of institutions of higher education, including the transnational (or exported) educational activities of institutions belonging to its member nations in Europe, Asia, and North America. The inaugural conference of the Global Alliance for Transnational Education (GATE) took place in London in the fall of 1996. GATE's brochure begins with familiar themes:

> The global marketplace and new technology are contributing to the rapid globalization of higher education. No longer is higher education provided solely within national borders. Transnational educational programs, provided both by the higher edu-

cation and corporate sectors, can be found in multiple forms, provided both electronically and in traditional forms. Issues of quality, purpose and responsibility abound in this new borderless educational arena and the time is ripe for a new international alliance of business, higher education and government dedicated to principled advocacy for transnational educational programs. This new alliance is GATE—the Global Alliance for Transnational Education.[6]

GATE includes among its founders individuals representing:

Intergovernment organizations
UNESCO and the OECD, the latter of which will jointly sponsor the 1997 GATE conference.

International organization
International Network of Quality Assurance Agencies in Higher Education.

National accrediting bodies
Committee of University Principals, Republic of South Africa; Commission d'evaluation de l'enseignement collegial, Canada; Chilean Accreditation Council; Secretaria de Educación Pública, México; National Council for Education Awards, Ireland; Academic Degrees Committee of the State Council, People's Republic of China; and the New Zealand Academic Audit Unit.

National higher education associations
Hungarian Rectors' Conference, American Association of Collegiate Registrars and Admissions Officers, The Laurasian Institution (Japan and the United States); Australian Education Office, and the American Council on Education.

Institutions with large off-shore program offerings
Open University, United Kingdom, and Monash University, Australia.

Initial sponsoring corporation
Jones International, Ltd.

---

[6]Global Alliance for Transnational Education (GATE), *Introductory Brochure* (Englewood, Co.: Global Alliance for Transnational Education, 1996).

Ambassadors of U.S. Higher Education

In the professions, a recent example of international accreditation is the 1989 agreement among the engineering accreditation bodies of Australia, Canada, Ireland, New Zealand, the United Kingdom, and the United States. Known as the "Washington Accord," the accrediting bodies agreed to recognize the substantial equivalence or comparability of their respective processes for accrediting engineering programs. These accrediting bodies can make recommendations to licensing authorities in their home countries that engineering programs in the other member countries be treated as equivalent.[7] The General Agreement on Trade and Services (GATS) of the World Trade Organization has begun to affect business as usual by encouraging the development of common educational standards, mutual recognition, and the liberalization of the licensing and certification processes by which professionals are allowed to practice. Traditional, nationalistic modes of quality assurance, including institutional and program accreditation, will inevitably work in conjunction with and/or give way to global forms of public protection and educational quality, beginning with professional education. Countries whose education systems are not based on rigorous standards of literally "world-class" quality further risk the replacement of their professional labor force by those from countries that have anticipated global mobility and fine-tuned their quality assurance systems accordingly.[8]

The Role of the Center for Quality Assurance in International Education

The author of this chapter is the executive director of the Center for Quality Assurance in International Education, a consortium of higher and international education associations and accrediting agencies located at the National Center for Higher Education in Washington, D.C. The center's purposes are essentially twofold: to promote quality in the globalization of U.S. higher education domestically and abroad, and to assist national systems in the reform of higher education with an emphasis on the role of quality assurance (generally known as accreditation in the United States). In fulfilling its role of assisting other

---

[7]Ascher, *New Trade Agreements*.
[8]Marjorie Peace Lenn, "Quality Assurance in Internationalization." Paper presented at Conference of Institutional Management in Higher Education (IMHE), of the Organization for Economic Cooperation and Development (OECD) (Monterey, Calif., 1995).

countries, with the exception of the European Rectors' regional accreditation initiative, the center has been involved directly in all the regional activities cited earlier. Further, for four years, the center has held an annual conference on trade agreements, higher education, and the emergence of global professions. Involving 25 key professions, the first three of these gatherings concentrated on the members of the North American Free Trade Agreement (NAFTA), while the most recent was held at the U.S. Department of State and included representatives from 15 countries and from the World Trade Organization, OECD, and the Asia Pacific Economic Cooperation.

The center's domestic agenda cannot be considered separately from its global activities. The center, a nonprofit education association, was formed in 1992 with a primary focus on the quality of U.S. credit-bearing programs offered abroad. In addition to assisting over 20 countries in the development of quality assurance policies and processes for their own higher education systems, the center has also assisted some of these same countries in policy development affecting foreign education provided within their borders. The following section of this chapter will outline the activities of the center that led to the drafting of the *Standards for U.S. Institutions Offering Credit-Bearing Programs Abroad.*[9] (See Chapter 8.)

Standards for U.S. Institutions Offering Credit-Bearing Programs Abroad: A Brief History

Activity bordering on the frenetic characterized the exploration of the globe's new frontiers by U.S. institutions of higher education in the late 1980s. Although "study-abroad" programs for U.S. students taking a portion of their academic degree in another country were familiar, not so familiar were institutions offering their credits and degrees to foreign nationals on their own shores. By the early 1990s even the (substantial) U.S. higher education offerings provided on military bases throughout the world were opened to foreign nationals for degree work. The primary locus of activity in the late 1980s and early 1990s was Asia—particularly Malaysia and Japan—expanding throughout Asia in subsequent years. When Eastern/Central Europe and Russia were liberated of past con-

---

[9]Center for Quality Assurance in International Education, *Standards for U.S. Institutions Offering Credit-Bearing Programs Abroad* (Washington, D.C.: Center for Quality Assurance in International Education, 1994).

straints, this section of the globe became one of the new frontiers along with Western Europe, which is infatuated with the U.S. Master's of Business Administration (M.B.A.). It is now thought (although not confirmed) that U.S. higher education programs can be found in credit-bearing form on every continent, and in large numbers.

Although there are programs offered by U.S. institutions of higher education of excellent quality worldwide, the movement has been plagued by programs with fewer virtues. Historically, most of the concerns about quality have rested in issues of *control.* (In his chapter on institutional accreditation, Steven Crow notes an evolution of issues concerning quality, originally emphasizing *control* but supplanted more recently by an emphasis on *evaluation.*) Many programs make arrangements to provide credits and degrees throughout the world without adequate consultation with the home campus. Particularly if there is a financially lucrative contract, institutions have been known to have memory lapses as to whom they are accountable in terms of governance and academic program planning. Sometimes faculty are recruited locally—or "off the streets"—to save time and money, giving rise to concerns about the quality of instruction. And often programs not offered at the home campus are initiated abroad, sometimes taught in the native language, thus giving rise to multiple issues of whether this is really U.S. higher education. Finally, there are a number of cases in which U.S. institutions naively or knowingly find themselves in countries in which foreign academic programs are either not welcomed or not sanctioned by the local government.

In 1994 the Center for Quality Assurance in International Education received a grant from the Test of English as a Foreign Language (TOEFL) Policy Council to host an invitational symposium in June of that year at the Chauncey Center at Educational Testing Service in Princeton, New Jersey. Entitled "Does U.S. Higher Education Need a Foreign Policy?" the symposium was attended by U.S. and international educational leaders and representatives from such intergovernment organizations as UNESCO and The Council of Europe. (A list of participants attending the June symposium, some of whom attended a planning meeting the following December, is found in Appendix 1.)

Clearly, the U.S. higher education system sets a global standard in terms of its resources, its diversity, and its accessibility. Yet for

≋ *Yet for all of this, there has been virtually no attempt to bring consistency and quality to the way in which our institutions of higher education relate to the rest of the world.*

all of this, there has been virtually no attempt to bring consistency and quality to the way in which our institutions of higher education relate to the rest of the world. Increasingly, the reputation and leadership of the U.S. higher education system is called into question by both students and educators in other countries due to a lack of clear and consistent thinking on international outreach on the part of the American higher education community. Examples abound which show the need for coordination and consistency on issues such as the mutual recognition of standards, credit transfer, development of linkages, relationship of branch campuses to the home campus, quality of study abroad programming, testing of foreign students entering our system, and other similar matters. These examples reinforce the most fundamental dictate of any foreign policy—that the actions of one will, inevitably, reflect on others.[10]

The symposium identified three key needs to adequately assure the educational quality of credit-bearing programs abroad:
  I. The need to identify the scope of the problem;
  II. The need to establish core standards for educational quality; and
  III. The need for a coordinated monitoring mechanism for educational quality.

Unknown Scope: The Problem and a Solution
At the core of the difficulty is the fact that U.S. higher education, even with its multiple national and international associations and its accrediting bodies, cannot provide an accurate count or the location of credit-bearing programs abroad. All that can be provided with certainty is a list of the modes by which the United States exports higher education. These include:

Distance-Education Programs
Programs delivered at a distance through satellites, computers, correspondence, and other technological means.

---

[10]Center for Quality Assurance in International Education, "Does U.S. Higher Education Need a Foreign Policy?" Position paper emanating from an invitational symposium made possible through a grant from the TOEFL Policy Council (Washington, D.C.: Center for Quality Assurance in Higher Education, 1994).

Study-Abroad Programs
International educational experiences of various duration for U.S. students as a part of their degree program in which foreign nationals are also involved. There are only educated guesses as to how many programs exist globally; most guesses approximate 1,000.

Single-Purpose Programs
There appears to be a global proliferation of educational programs focusing on specific professions, such as the M.B.A. and graduate programs in engineering.

Branch Campuses
Credit-bearing, including degree-granting programs offered by U.S.-based institutions of higher education targeting foreign nationals in their own countries.

Institutions Chartered in the United States but Operating Abroad
Degree-granting programs, many of which were established for the American expatriot community but which now serve predominantly foreign national student bodies.

Educational Programs on Military Bases
It is estimated that 371 U.S. institutions of higher education provide credit-generating programs leading to degrees at 171 military bases around the world. These programs were opened in recent years to foreign nationals.

Educational "Linkage" or "Twinning" Programs
Untold numbers of formal and informal agreements exist between U.S. and foreign institutions for joint program/degree offerings.

English as a Second Language (ESL) Programs
ESL and other programs that often do not carry academic credit but that act as ambassadors for U.S. higher education to foreign nationals.

At the least, it is important that U.S. higher education account for where it is operating, in what form, for what purpose, and in what population. To date, the U.S. position on exportation has been based on a "whatever the market will bear" mentality without full regard for producing quality products. In an attempt to devise a method of accounting, GATE plans as one of its primary services to provide a current data base of all educational programs that have crossed borders and that have undergone a process of evaluation by a formal evaluating body. This data base, to be compiled by the American Association of Collegiate Registrars and Admissions Officers (AACRAO) for GATE, will list all such transnational educational programs provided by any country anywhere. It will be the first available listing of its kind.

Core Standards for Educational Quality: The Problem and a Solution

There do not exist core standards of educational quality by which U.S. institutions can readily evaluate their international programs. Instead, several sets of "standards" are available that institutions can voluntarily apply to their programs abroad. A sample list of sources for these standards is found in Appendix 2. The standards come in various forms, some directly applicable to international programs, such as principles of good practice, guidelines, executive orders, advisory lists, etc. Others are only indirectly applicable, such as institutional or specialized accrediting standards (i.e., indirect in that, with one or two exceptions, accrediting standards are not intended to be specific to an exported educational product). The sources of these standards are as varied as the standards themselves, ranging from government bodies such as state coordinating agencies to international educational associations. Further, there has been little coordination among international associations, states, accrediting agencies, and other bodies in the formulation of such standards. Institutions are, therefore, left to their own devices to best guess which standards are most important.

Confronted with this dilemma, those gathered for the symposium and subsequent planning meeting drafted a set of *Standards for U.S. Institutions Offering Credit-Bearing Programs Abroad* to be used by institutions, programs, associations, and accrediting bodies in their internal and/or external review processes. After the standards were proposed in 1994, the drafters met with a wide variety of constituencies at the annual meetings of such organizations as the College Board, the American Association of Collegiate Registrars and Admissions Officers, the Association of International Education Administrators, the Association of Specialized and Professional Accreditors, the European Association of International Education, and OECD. (The standards are presented in Chapter 8.)

A Coordinated Monitoring Mechanism for Educational Quality: The Problem and a Solution

There is little coordination in U.S. higher education between those agencies formally charged with assuring quality and the international education bodies that promote and nurture the exportation of our educational products. Further, the regional institutional accrediting agencies do not share common processes and procedures for monitoring the quality of higher education nationally, much less internationally. While there is a growing consensus on the need to apply core standards consistently, what the mechanism should be remains a question. This problem is not new. Off-campus educational programs have historically challenged traditional modes of evaluation, including accreditation. Several years ago, the various branches of the armed forces assumed responsibility for ensuring the quality of the education offered on U.S. military bases throughout the world when regional accreditation bodies were unresponsive. And in distance education, state authorizing agencies and accrediting bodies have sought over the years to identify an effective process for evaluating an educational delivery system that defies traditional models.

At the very least, a coordinated effort is needed among evaluating and authorizing entities to agree on core standards, unless they wish to forfeit this responsibility sooner rather than later to what will inevitably become an international process. But then, perhaps an international evaluation process makes the most sense, given the evolving nature of transnational educational programs, in which both the context and the students are different from those for which our national formal evaluation systems were designed. Countries such as Hungary, Estonia, Korea, Singapore, Hong Kong, and China have established national policies for educational programs from other countries operating within their borders.

GATE, the alliance of government, business, and higher education associations described earlier, is developing principles of good practice for credit-bearing programs that are not unlike the standards proposed in this book. The GATE principles were piloted in the fall of 1996 through the evaluation of a number of Australian higher education off-

≈≈ There is little coordination in U.S. higher education between those agencies formally charged with assuring quality and the international education bodies that promote and nurture the exportation of our educational products.

shore offerings. The Center for Quality Assurance in International Education has been asked to coordinate the activities of this new global alliance. Its board and staff have accepted this responsibility readily in the knowledge that international cooperation on matters related to educational programs that cross national borders is most probably the soundest of current alternatives for assuring their quality. U.S. institutions, higher education associations, and accrediting bodies not already a part of this movement are encouraged to join their international colleagues in the effort to ensure quality programs abroad.

Dr. Marjorie Peace Lenn is the founding executive director of the Center for Quality Assurance in International Education and the executive director of the Global Alliance for Transnational Education located at the National Center for Higher Education in Washington, D.C. A former administrator at the University of Massachusetts and vice president of the Council on Postsecondary Accreditation, Dr. Lenn speaks and publishes extensively on issues of quality in higher education internationally. She leads programs and/or serves in an advising capacity for numerous international organizations, including the World Bank, the United Nations Educational, Scientific, and Cultural Organization, the Organization of American States, the Council of Europe, the Organization of Economic Cooperation and Development, and the International Network of Quality Assurance Agencies in Higher Education.

CHAPTER 3

Institutional Accreditation and the International Offering of Credit-Bearing Courses and Degree Programs

Steven D. Crow
North Central Association of Colleges and Schools

Associations that provide institutional accreditation typically claim that their process "evaluates an entire institution and accredits it as a whole."[1] When U.S. institutions of higher education began to deliver courses and programs off campus, the accrediting community quickly started monitoring them, claiming that the accreditors had to vouch for the quality of the education an institution offered, wherever the education was provided. Some accrediting associations required approval of off-campus programs before they commenced; others required follow-up review after they were introduced. Whatever the monitoring strategy, each association accepted responsibility for evaluating the quality of off-campus offerings.

Today, the law requires that federally recognized accrediting associations closely monitor institutions that establish branch campuses. Department of Education policy extends that law to include sites at which 50 percent or more of a degree program is offered. Regional accrediting associations continue to refine their policies and procedures for evaluating off-campus education. As the national map of higher education becomes a delicately intricate fretwork of lines connecting courses and programs to sponsoring institutions, regional associations are working to strengthen the consistency and congruency of their various approaches to off-campus education.

Until the mid-1980s, accreditors usually evaluated courses and programs offered in international settings under the same umbrella of policies and procedures they applied to domestic off-campus offerings. To some extent that approach made sense. For several decades, U.S. institutions of higher education had transported their credit courses and degree programs to international settings. With the exception of

---

[1]North Central Association of Colleges and Schools, *Handbook of Accreditation 1994–96*, p. 1 (North Central Association of Colleges and Schools, 1994).

students attending unique U.S.-chartered foreign-based institutions such as the American University of Paris or the American University in Cairo, the students who took advantage of these offerings were primarily Americans, among whom were study-abroad students, military personnel and their dependents, and religious and business expatriates. For these students, international offerings simply attempted to replicate home-campus courses and programs. Students might be living in a different culture, but for the most part their approach to education was shaped by the U.S. culture out of which they came. The basic expectation for off-campus education, whether 100 miles away or an ocean away, was that it duplicate as closely as possible the education offered at the home campus.

In the mid-1980s, however, regional accrediting associations began to recognize the inadequacy of this accrediting model for addressing the new trends in international education. As Marjorie Peace Lenn illustrated, a rich variety of ventures came to mark the international educational scene and the involvement of U.S. institutions in it. Not only did the market for U.S. offerings shift from U.S. students to foreign nationals, but the business and contractual relationships undergirding U.S. enterprises usually involved foreign nationals as well. Typically through a contract with a foreign corporation, U.S. institutions agreed to deliver "American-style" education with course and degree content somewhat different from that offered at the home campus. Some repackaged their curricula into modular, short-term offerings, and expected their U.S. faculty to travel abroad during breaks and vacations to deliver the courses. Some U.S. institutions encouraged the development of private enterprises that offered American-style programs under the aegis of a U.S. college or university. The U.S. institution then either granted its credit for the courses or accepted in transfer the credits earned in the program. The physical settings for these offerings varied greatly.

If accreditors thought they could monitor these new initiatives simply by reviewing institutional documents to find evidence that home-campus courses and programs were being duly replicated, they soon learned otherwise. Institutions did their best to follow the replicate/duplicate paradigm, but actual practice inevitably involved multiple compromises to accommodate the international context. International site visits, once thought to be a thin excuse for an all-expense-paid junket, became more and more common as accrediting associations sought to understand the real scope and nature of U.S. involvement in international education. At times the task at hand, vouching for the educational offerings of an institution as a whole, seemed so jeopardized by these new international endeavors that some accrediting associations gave serious consideration to the position that "accreditation halts at the water's edge." In 1989 the Council on Postsecondary Accreditation (COPA), at that time the membership association of accrediting agencies, said that accreditors could not sidestep taking responsibility for assessing the quality of the education institutions provided in international settings.

With the exception of a few notable collaborative efforts during the late 1960s and early 1970s, regional accrediting associations independently developed their own policies and procedures. Anyone who studies the policies of the regional associations will find a significant similarity of interests and concerns as well as some striking differences. Even though those differences became more and more marked in the 1980s, the regionals understood that in responding to these new international ventures they needed to find some common ground. Historians concerned with recognizing initial movers and causal leadership can mine the documents of the various regionals and COPA to identify them. The fact is, however, that under the aegis of COPA, the executive directors of the regional associations endorsed on February 14, 1990, the basic components of *Principles of Good Practice in Overseas International Education Programs for Non-U.S. Nationals.*[2] The regional associations adopted these principles as their own.

In its emphasis on the contractual nature of most recent international efforts, *Principles of Good Practice* highlighted some very important considerations then unfamiliar to most U.S. institutions. In its willingness to encourage education relevant to different cultural settings, *Principles of Good Practice* provided a useful new alternative to the replicate/duplicate paradigm. By emphasizing the U.S. institution's obligations to its international constituents, it brought home the central challenge of institutional integrity in these new settings. Many institutions just

---

[2]Council on Postsecondary Accreditation (COPA), Regional Institutional Accrediting Bodies (Washington, D.C.: Council on Postsecondary Education, Regional Institutional Accrediting Bodies, 1990).

beginning to consider the initiation of international programs have used the principles to great benefit. Over the past half-decade, a series of international evaluation visits conducted by the regional associations has been informed by the evaluation strategies embedded in the principles. The principles were first and foremost the product of accreditors, and reflected their best efforts at responding to a new and dynamic challenge. But as with any document that attempts during a time of rapid change to define good practice and provide a yardstick for evaluation, the COPA document was probably dated almost before it was published.

The Center for Quality Assurance in International Education provided, through its project A Foreign Policy for U.S. Higher Education, the opportunity for a series of discussions that ultimately led to the set of standards presented in this volume. While the voices of regional accrediting associations were heard in this project, many other individuals and organizations engaged in international education sought to address in the project their own experiences and concerns.

The purpose of this chapter is not to argue the merits of the two documents, for in many respects they address similar concerns. Institutions contemplating the initiation or evaluation of international educational operations would be well served to study both. But the standards not only represent the thoughts and experiences of a broader constituency; they also reflect some of the changing thinking about issues of quality assurance in U.S. educational activities abroad.

Educational Objectives in International Programs
Accreditors expect institutions to find within their mission and purposes a rationale for international offerings. U.S. institutions have given many different reasons for engaging in international ventures. Only a few have stated baldly that the objective was to tap new sources of revenue, although almost none expected the international endeavor to actually cost them significant dollars. Most explained that these international activities would contribute to the globalization of U.S. higher education by (1) opening a new avenue through which foreign nationals would be prepared for study in the United States, and (2) expanding the ability of U.S. faculty, through experience teaching abroad, to bring to the U.S. curriculum a much-needed global perspective.

The standards affirm the tenet that an institution's international educational offerings should be clearly related to its mission and purposes.

But by focusing on the goals and objectives of the course/program offerings, the standards also propose that institutions should address clearly the relationship between the education they propose to offer abroad, the educational needs of international students, and the educational context of the host country. For example, it is not clear that the international students who pay the bills always benefit as much as they expected from taking U.S. courses and programs. In non-English-speaking nations, to be more specific, U.S. institutions have almost always underestimated the difficulty of providing an effective enough ESL program to ensure that students can matriculate in English-language courses/programs. Institutional reputations—and the reputation of U.S. higher education—rise and fall on the success of ESL programs, not on the content of regular degree programs. In countries where the basic reward system—jobs, salary, status—is heavily geared to the relative prestige of the institutions of higher education within the host country, U.S. education is often viewed as being somewhat second-rate. If completed in the United States, a U.S. degree often carries some weight within the international community in the host country, but when completed without any educational experience in the United States at all, the degree clearly strikes many in the host country as markedly inferior.

This is not to suggest that U.S. institutions have no role to play in international settings; rather, it says that they should understand clearly the relationship between the education they propose to offer and the use international students reasonably can expect to make of that education. Every U.S. institution needs to enhance the global perspective in its curricula; recruiting and educating international students, whether at the home campus or abroad, is one way to accomplish that goal. International students, however, must have their own unique educational objectives and needs fulfilled even as they contribute to heightened global awareness at U.S. institutions.

Faculty in International Settings

Everyone agrees that faculty in international settings should possess the appropriate academic credentials and language proficiencies necessary for effective instruction. Everyone expects U.S. standards to prevail; for example, faculty at international sites should possess graduate degrees in the appropriate disciplines. But experience suggests that other significant issues are involved, especially when one looks carefully at the international faculty's role in quality assurance. The standards, therefore, emphasize other priorities to consider.

U.S. education involves a culture of learning that is often distinctly different from that found in many other nations. The centrality of faculty-student interaction and student-student interaction should be captured in international settings, whether the education is being provided by U.S. institutions or, under their oversight, in institutions providing American-style education. The effort to stimulate students to be active participants in the learning process should be integral to the educational experience, particularly for students intending to transfer to or continue education in the United States. The American practice of frequent monitoring of learning (through periodic oral and written examinations, oral presentations, and/or assigned essays) should be honored. In many cultures, students find these practices very foreign indeed. And some faculty educated in other English-speaking countries find them equally foreign. U.S. institutions must recruit credentialed, English-speaking faculty for their international offerings, but if they want their international students to be prepared for further education in the United States, they need to ensure that students actually experience the culture of learning they will encounter in the United States.

While many applaud the U.S. institutions that send their own faculty abroad, it is clear that not all faculty are equally well-prepared to teach in international contexts. Several U.S. faculty have discovered that teaching styles that appeared to be well-received in the United States simply did not work well abroad. Moreover, some institutions penalize those who are very effective instructors abroad simply by relying on tenure and promotion systems that do not give full weight to such experiences. Too often, because institutions have not carefully thought through the central importance of the faculty to the success of students, U.S. operations abroad are marked by a rapid turnover in faculty. Not only does this contribute to a lack of continuity in instruction that would not be tolerated on most U.S. campuses, but international students are exposed to too much "learning on the job" when faculty are unfamiliar with the culture from which their students come. Because most home-campus academic administrators are unfamiliar with the special teaching needs in international settings, repeated emphasis on their need to "control" international programs misses the most critical objective—ensuring effective teaching.

Institutional Evaluation/Assessment in International Settings

The standards reflect the emergence in U.S. higher education of a focus on student learning. If institutions offering courses and programs in international settings need to appreciate the educational requirements and cultural backgrounds of students, if those institutions also need to pay greater attention to the fit between the faculty and the cultures of learning of those students, then they also need systems of evaluation and assessment that provide assurance that the students are actually mastering what they are being taught.

Program review is one component of a multifaceted evaluation procedure, and in it usually resides some measure of student academic achievement. It stands to reason, then, that program review is very important in international settings. It stands to reason as well that the home institution should include international offerings within its ongoing evaluation procedures, whether they are conducted by discipline, department, or school.

As institutions develop and implement procedures by which they assess student learning, those, too, should be extended to international programs. The objective of this is not simply to ensure that "the standard of student achievement in the international program is equivalent to the standard of student achievement on the U.S. campus,"[3] although that should remain a solid measure of educational quality. The objective also should be to encourage those most intimately involved in the international program to learn to assess student learning more effectively and thereby strengthen and enhance courses/programs. Evaluation and assessment procedures, then, need to involve the international faculty and administration, not just the home campus.

In defining the key tools for quality assurance in international educational ventures, the *Principles of Good Practice* placed significant emphasis on the ability of the U.S. institution to "control" the international courses or program. The standards continue to assume that the home institution bears the major responsibility for oversight of its international operations. But the shift in language between the two documents from "control" to "evaluation" is worth noting. Excellence in international education requires a clear vision of educational objectives, a

---

[3]Id.

≋ As institutions develop and implement procedures by which they assess student learning, those, too, should be extended to international programs.

strong commitment to those charged with implementing that vision, and a sound system of evaluation. Excellence also requires that the home institution have the willingness to learn from its experiences and to strengthen as necessary its support to ensure that students abroad learn what is taught. "Control" suggests, although it does not require, a one-way street, with the home institution as the locus of all wisdom. "Evaluation" proposes a more synergistic paradigm, suggesting that the home institution, if it focuses appropriately on the learning experiences of its students in international settings, will be open itself to the changes that result from the learning experiences embedded in every international educational venture.

Steven D. Crow joined the Commission on Institutions of Higher Education of the North Central Association of Colleges and Schools in 1982 after a decade of college teaching. He assumed the title of acting executive director on January 1, 1997.

CHAPTER 4

International Considerations in Program Accreditation

John Maudlin-Jeronimo
Executive Director
National Architectural Accrediting Board

Accreditation signifies that an institution or program meets an established standard of educational achievement. Its purpose is to maintain and enhance, beyond minimum threshold standards, the quality of educational performance, and to better serve and safeguard the public. The achievement of these goals is ascertained by an evaluation process carried out by voluntary associations of educators and professional practitioners.

In the United States, accreditation in higher education is conducted at both the institutional and program levels. Institutional accreditation, conducted by voluntary associations of institutions in various geographic regions, reviews the entire educational institution and focuses on institutional processes and operating procedures. Program accreditation is conducted for individual disciplines (law, music, medicine, etc.) by associations of educators and professional practitioners.

Program accreditation in the United States can be categorized as either professional or specialized. Professions that are regulated by states through licensure or certification (law, medicine, architecture, etc.) require applicants to be graduates of professionally accredited programs. Nonregulated disciplines (music, fine arts, journalism, etc.) voluntarily participate in specialized accreditation.

The U.S. system of professional accreditation is a direct outgrowth of the U.S. system of professional education and the tradition of state regulation of professional services. Thomas Jefferson, the third president of the United States, was the architect of the University of Virginia and founded it in 1819. Jefferson was a lawyer educated in the law through the traditional apprenticeship system. He came to believe that access to the professions should not be through apprenticeships, which relied on financial or political influence for entry, but through university education open to those individuals with the necessary intellectual capabilities. Jefferson proposed that all students aspiring to a professional career complete a foundation program in the liberal arts or the great books followed by study in one of the professional disciplines. His proposal put a pedagogy for a U.S. system of professional education into place.

The mid-1800s saw the organization and growth of national professional societies and associations. In 1844 the American Institute of Homeopathy was founded, followed by the American Medical Association in 1847, the American Society of Civil Engineers and the American Pharmaceutical Association in 1852, the American Institute of Architects in 1857, and the American Dental Association in 1859.

In 1862 the Morrill Land-Grant Act was passed to provide federal funding to states "to promote the liberal and practical education of the industrial classes in the several pursuits and professions."[1]

The progressive movement in the late 1800s led to the public's awareness of and concern for product and services safety. Laws were passed to control the meat packing industry, and work place safety regulations and housing and building codes were enacted. States accepted not only their right but their responsibility to enact laws and regulations for the protection of the public's health, safety, and welfare.

The first state law regulating a profession was enacted in 1859 in North Carolina to license and register physicians. By the turn of the century, most professions were licensed in at least some states.

Program Accreditation in the United States

In the United States, the regulation (licensure, registration, and certification) of the professions is a function of the police power of the separate states. The federal government does not regulate professions in this country. However, due to the influence of national voluntary professional societies and associations, individual state laws and regulations are very similar within each profession.

State laws and regulations require at least two criteria for licensure: the meeting of some minimum educational standard, and the passing of

---

[1] *The Architect at Mid-Century* (Washington, D.C.: AIA Press, 1951).

Ambassadors of U.S. Higher Education

a state licensing examination. Some professions also require an internship period.

In the early years of professional licensing, the mere participation of professional schools or faculty of the schools in professional societies or associations was considered an acceptable demonstration that a school met the minimum educational standard. As the number of schools grew in some professions, national organizations of schools were founded and membership in those organizations was considered to meet the educational standard. As growth and complexity overtook professional education, the responsibility for establishing and evaluating standards of educational achievement was passed to independent organizations: the accrediting agencies.

Both professional and specialized accreditation are national in scope. States accept graduates of programs accredited by national agencies as meeting the states' standards. The national accrediting agencies are nongovernmental. They are supported by national professional and educational societies, organizations of each profession, and fees from schools.

The governing board of an accrediting agency is either elected or appointed by the national professional societies and organizations of the discipline, and includes representatives from both academia and practice. Most boards include representatives of the public and some include students. It is the governing board that makes the decision on a program's accreditation.

In all but a few cases, the agency's governing board establishes the standards of educational achievement and the processes and procedures to be used in assessment. In some disciplines, however, the standards of educational achievement are established by the national educational organizations or professional societies, and the accrediting agency's governing board is empowered with authority to evaluate compliance with those standards and determine accreditation status.

The accreditation process for both professional and specialized programs requires a self-evaluation by the program to demonstrate compliance with the agency's standards, and then an external evaluation of the self-evaluation documentation by the agency, followed by an on-site review conducted by a team representing the agency. The review is submitted to the agency's governing board for the decision regarding accreditation.

Accrediting agencies are required to present clear and accurate documentation of their standards and procedures to programs, institutions, and the public. Agencies provide assistance to programs in various ways: they help programs develop their self-evaluation documentation, they help programs prepare for the on-site visit by conducting workshops, and they provide format guidelines and handbooks as well as other materials.

Standards of educational achievement have three principle components: processes and procedures, context, and content. Processes and procedures refer to a program's operating guidelines. How is curriculum modified; how are courses developed and added? What are the procedures for student admission and how are the admission standards determined? Context includes human, physical, informational, and financial resources; the program and institutional setting and mission; and the objectives and ideals of the institution.

Content is the heart of all professional and specialized accreditation standards. What is the learning program that must be mastered by students for the program to be accredited? Content distinguishes one profession from another and content defines professions and specializations. While the body of knowledge of any profession is definable, it is beyond the capacity and time available for any program to include everything. The imperative is to define the critical core of the body of knowledge that all participants in the process—educators, practitioners, students, and the public—agree must be part of formal education in the profession.

The Accreditation Process
For a program to meet minimum accreditation standards, it must demonstrate that students have achieved the established level of competence in each area of the critical core of the program. A program cannot choose to eliminate one element of the critical core and emphasize or specialize in another. The critical core of the body of knowledge is how that profession has defined itself, and all graduates who wish to enter that profession must possess that knowledge.

The on-site team visit, coupled with the program's self-evaluation documentation, provides the information necessary for a team to make a judgment on the program's compliance with agency standards. Teams, usually from three to six persons, are nominated by the agency's governing board, and always include both educators and practitioners from the discipline or profession with an understanding of or experience in the accreditation process. Programs can usually add school-nominated observers to the team.

The visit lasts three to four days and is structured around the team's need to gather information. Meetings are held with the institution's academic leaders, other administrators, program administrators, faculty, students, recent graduates, and other alumni. The facilities and learning resources are toured and evaluated. Both faculty and students engage in presentations and discussions about the program and students' work.

The team's first responsibility is to write a report on its findings for the program's use and for the agency's governing board so the board can make a decision on the program's accreditation status. The accreditation of the program is dependent on a judgment that the program meets the minimum standards of educational achievement.

No team and no accrediting agency, however, wants the process to be confined simply to the assessment of achieving minimum standards. Programs that merely aspire to mediocrity do not contribute to their discipline, profession, or to society.

The second and a critical component of the process of accreditation is program enhancement. Visiting accreditation teams are, in fact, external independent peer review teams. So while they carry out their first responsibility, to evaluate compliance with minimum standards, they also provide programs with their assessment of opportunities for program development and improvement. Clearly establishing and articulating the critical core of a discipline or profession and ensuring its mastery provides the best opportunity for strength as well as diversity in program focus. Visiting teams explore with programs their strengths and the potential opportunities to capitalize on faculty interests, location, and institutional mission. It is a goal of each accreditation team to see the program maximize its uniqueness and develop its own character, which in turn leads to the greatest possible diversity of professional educational opportunities for students.

The Code of Good Practice

Professional accreditation differs somewhat from specialized accreditation because, in some cases, professional accreditation relies more heavily on practitioners and representatives of state licensing or regis-

≋ These factors have created interest in the development of agreements between professions of different countries to foster the mobility and reciprocal recognition of students, faculty, and practitioners.

tration boards in the accreditation process. Both professional and specialized program accreditation agencies, however, share common ideals and objectives for accreditation and have adopted, through the Association of Specialized and Professional Accreditors, the following Code of Good Practice:

An accrediting organization:

1. Pursues its mission, goals, and objectives, and conducts its operations in a trustworthy manner.

2. Maximizes service, productivity, and effectiveness in the accreditation relationship.

3. Respects and protects institutional autonomy.

4. Maintains a broad perspective as the basis for wise decision making.

5. Focuses accreditation reviews on the development of knowledge and competence.

6. Exhibits integrity and professionalism in the conduct of its operations.

7. Has mechanisms to ensure that expertise and experience in the application of its standards, procedures, and values are present in members of its visiting teams, commissions, and staff.[2]

The efforts of professional and specialized accrediting agencies to refine and improve their own standards and procedures and to attract dedicated, respected, and knowledgeable volunteers and staff foster a climate within the higher education community for improvement and quality enhancement. The purpose of accreditation is to ensure the maintenance and enhancement of an appropriate educational foundation in the various disciplines and professions. The aggregate national effect of this effort will ensure the maximum opportunity for student success and, ultimately, professionals who are not only qualified but considered excellent in their respective fields.

---

[2]Illinois: The Association of Specialized and Professional Accreditors, 1995.

International Initiatives

The U.S. system of accreditation certifies that an institution or program meets a minimum standard of educational achievement, which in turn facilitates the mobility of its graduates among all 50 states. Further, it is a nongovernment, nonfederal system that relies on members of the profession or discipline for support, leadership, and standard setting. These factors have created interest in the U.S. system among professions and professional schools outside the United States with respect to the improvement of the education and accreditation systems within their own countries and the development of agreements between professions of different countries to foster the mobility and reciprocal recognition of students, faculty, and practitioners.

American higher education has had an international component for many years and a number of professions have promoted the international mobility of practices and practitioners. Since World War II, most U.S. campuses have had their cadre of foreign students. Many colleges and universities and their affiliated professional schools offer overseas semesters for U.S. students, and in recent years U.S. institutions have offered degree programs overseas.

U.S. education in the fine and performing arts and in architecture and the decorative arts has strong and direct linkages to Western traditions developed in Europe. Many art and architecture programs provide opportunities to study the roots of these traditions in study-abroad programs.

The 1980s saw tremendous growth in overseas programs in business and international management education. U.S. business schools offered M.B.A. programs at overseas institutions taught by the faculty of those institutions. Learning alliances were formed among groups of U.S. and foreign institutions to offer degree and certificate programs both overseas and at home.

Two factors, the end of the cold war with the adoption and growth of market economies in former Soviet Bloc countries and the rapid development and growth in information and communication technologies, have opened new and exciting opportunities. The world is the marketplace, and access to qualified providers is the issue.

The United States has recognized that its economic future is in a strong information and service sector. All recent trade agreements have promoted the free access not only of goods but of services as well. The

≋ *The North American Free Trade Agreement (NAFTA) and the General Agreement on Trade and Services (GATS) require that the licensing of professionals be based on fair, objective, and transparent criteria and that permanent residency and citizenship requirements be abolished.*

U.S.–Canadian Free Trade Agreement included an "Architectural Annex," which committed both countries to work toward common standards for education and accreditation, licensure, and ethical practice. (In a trade agreement, an Annex is a subtext that clarifies a point.)

One option adopted by some professions for the accreditation of professional programs has been the establishment of a single common accreditation agency to review programs in more than one country. Architecture chose a different course.

In 1985 the School of Architecture at the University of British Columbia faced proposed closure by the university's president. While a series of events and factors led to his decision not to close the school, he did require the program to demonstrate that it was of significant quality to continue to serve its students and the province of British Columbia. The U.S. accrediting agency in architecture, the National Architectural Accrediting Board (NAAB), was requested by the School of Architecture to conduct a review of the school and its professional program based on U.S. standards.

The positive result of the NAAB review led to a request by the president of the University of British Columbia for NAAB accreditation of the architecture program. NAAB and the collateral organizations that represent U.S. architectural schools, professionals, state registration boards, and students formed a task force that reviewed the request and proposed a policy, not to accredit Canadian architecture programs but to assist Canada in establishing an accreditation system that paralleled NAAB's. The policy was adopted by the NAAB board.

Over the past decade, NAAB has worked with the Canadian Architectural Certification Board (CACB) to develop parallel accreditation systems. CACB adopted the NAAB standard for the definition of the content of an architect's education and its critical core, as well as comparable procedures for their evaluation. Observers from NAAB and CACB attended each others' board meetings, staffs conducted interagency office visits, members of the CACB board were observers on NAAB accreditation visits, and all CACB accreditation visit teams to Canadian schools included a member representing NAAB.

In the spring of 1996 the accreditation of all architecture programs in Canada was completed. Ironically, the last school visited was that at the University of British Columbia. Canada and the United States have entered into an agreement that recognizes NAAB and CACB accredited degree programs as equivalent for purposes of licensure and registration in the states and provinces of the United States and Canada.

The North American Free Trade Agreement (NAFTA) and the General Agreement on Trade and Services (GATS) require that the licensing of professionals be based on fair, objective, and transparent criteria and that permanent residency and citizenship requirements be abolished. These trade agreements force professions to look beyond their own borders for the definition of their profession and its common core of knowledge. This fosters a need for a coordinated process of quality assurance governed by a common code of good practices.

Core standards and the harmonization of standards are not one and the same. Harmonization requires all participants to adopt a common standard and to have the same regulations and procedures. Most professions, especially those with a strong cultural and location context, seek to develop core standards that define the minimum content all participants agree is necessary for education and practice.

Professions adopting the core standards concept to meet the requirements of bilateral or multilateral agreements under NAFTA or GATS must develop a coordinated process to ensure the comparability and convertibility of standards and credentials. If a degree program is to meet the core standards requirement, an assessment of how its content compares with the requirement of the other jurisdiction is made and how the degree holder can convert the credential for licensure and practice in the other jurisdiction is determined.

Opportunities must be opened to fill any gaps in a person's education or experience that prevent him or her from being licensed and able to practice in another country. Professional development programs and continuing educational opportunities offered by educational institutions, professional associations, and individual providers must become part of a profession's system of quality assurance. The need for multinational post-professional educational opportunities will certainly provide some incentive for the development of distance learning programs but will in turn require that those providers be part of a recognized quality assurance system.

In the spirit of both NAFTA and GATS, NAAB and the Royal Institute of British Architects were invited by the Architectural Society of China to make presentations to the deans of the schools of architecture in

≈≈ What we envision is a variety of systems, national, continental, and multi-national, not with the same standards and procedures but with differing criteria and processes that respect and are influenced by culture, location, and common practice and that all meet the international minimum standard.

China on accreditation. In 1990 China adopted the NAAB system of architectural accreditation and asked for NAAB assistance in establishing it in China. NAAB over the past few years has hosted observers from China on NAAB on-site reviews and NAAB representatives have served as observers on architectural accreditation visits in China and partic-ipated in their accreditation symposiums following the visits.

In both Colombia and Chile, NAAB has made a "mock" accreditation visit to a school of architecture at the school's request. The mock visit required a school to conduct a self-study demonstrating its compliance with NAAB standards, an on-site visit that followed the typical NAAB visit agenda, a presentation of team findings prior to departure from the school, and a final written Visiting Team Report. The only difference between a mock visit and a typical NAAB visit is that while the NAAB board receives the Visiting Team Report for informational purposes, it takes no accreditation action on it.

In the case of Chile, the school of architecture visited is leading the effort to establish a system of accreditation to improve the quality of architectural education in Chile and, ultimately, to improve the quality of Chile's built environment.

This past year NAAB was again requested to accredit a non-U.S. program in architecture. NAAB affirmed a policy not to accredit non-U.S. programs but to work toward the international exchange of information and the coordination of common standards by helping countries or groups of countries establish architectural accrediting systems that are both comparable and convertible.

The Union of International Architects, which is composed of all the national architectural societies, began an effort in 1995 to develop by 1999 a proposal for an "Accord on International Minimum Standards of Professionalism in Architectural Practice," which will include standards for both education and accreditation.

What we envision is a variety of systems, national, continental, and multinational, not with the same standards and procedures but with dif-fering criteria and processes that respect and are influenced by culture, location, and common practice and that all meet the international minimum standard. In architecture as in other professions and disci-plines, we are united by the sharing of a fundamental core definition of our profession and its responsibilities to society. While our vision is

Ambassadors of U.S. Higher Education

broadened and our profession enriched by our differences and diversity, through accreditation we can assure the commonality but also celebrate the plurality of our profession.

John Maudlin-Jeronimo is an architect and a certified association executive. A member of the College of Fellows of the American Institute of Architects, he is the executive director of the National Architectural Accrediting Board and chairman of the board of the Center for Quality Assurance in International Education.

CHAPTER 5

Case Study:
Maintaining and Controlling Academic Standards at U.S. Branch Campuses in Japan

Jared H. Dorn, Director
Southern Illinois University at Carbondale in Niigata, Japan

For a number of reasons, the phenomenon of U.S. branch-campus development in Japan is of interest to educators. Its explosive nature, the number and diversity of U.S. institutions and Japanese partners involved, its relationship to larger binational issues of trade and exchange, its exposure of vast culturally related differences in expectations and communication styles, the drama associated with some abrupt branch-campus closings, and its rather short history are among the intriguing aspects of the phenomenon. For those interested in the maintenance and control of academic standards in U.S. credit-bearing programs abroad, the U.S.-Japanese experience offers some instructive case histories.

History of the Branch-Campus Movement in Japan
There was a proliferation of plans by U.S. colleges and universities to deliver credit-bearing programs in Japan between 1987 and 1990. *Profiting from Education: Japan-United States International Educational Ventures in the 1980s*, the insightful study by Chambers and Cummings published in 1990, estimated that over 100 U.S. institutions had actually sent representatives to explore branch-campus possibilities.[1] Many of these institutions presumably held hopes for delivering credit courses. The majority, however, never developed concrete plans or realized branch campuses in Japan. And, although at least 30 institutions did establish branch campuses in partnerships with Japanese interests during this period, most of them never reached the point of delivering a significant number of credit courses.

The realities of the English-language competency of Japanese students meant that all but a few branch campuses initially had to offer an

---

[1]Gail S. Chambers and William K. Cummings, *Profiting from Education: Japan-United States International Educational Ventures in the 1980s* (New York: Institute of International Education, 1990).

≋ *In the late 1980s several factors contributed to the branch-campus movement, including keen interest in U.S. higher education among young people, an enthusiasm that persists.*

extensive period of intensive English-language instruction for the vast majority of their students. Most of this was not credit bearing. A few programs, those in which the Japanese partners exerted strong influence on academic affairs, offered entering students a combination of credit courses taught primarily in Japanese along with semi-intensive English-language instruction. These programs were met with apprehension and criticism from branch campuses conducting credit-bearing programs only in English and from other concerned parties.

In the late 1980s several factors contributed to the branch-campus movement, including keen interest in U.S. higher education among young people, an enthusiasm that persists, as indicated by the steady increase in Japanese enrollment at U.S. colleges and universities.[2] At that time, many Japanese students and their families were still unfamiliar with the various avenues to, and fearful of direct entry into, U.S. higher education. In addition, there was growing dissatisfaction with the rigidity and the entrance examination system of Japanese higher education. There was also a thrust from government and private sector forces in Japan toward internationalization, resulting in many activities of mixed motives cloaked in international slogans. Finally, that was the period of the so-called "bubble economy," and Japanese public and private interests were eager for adventure and able to take unprecedented risks.

The environment in Japan for branch campuses was at first welcoming, in general. One large U.S. public university had operated a branch campus in Tokyo in private partnerships for half a decade when, in 1986, the U.S.-Japan Committee for Promoting Trade Expansion, formed by 20 U.S. Congressmen and 10 Japanese Diet members, introduced an initiative to bring U.S. academic programs to Japan. Public and private Japanese interests issued open invitations and, in the autumn of 1986, U.S. university representatives began meeting in Washington, D.C. and elsewhere to explore the feasibility of responding. On the Japanese side, national political figures such as Diet members Susumu Nikaido and Yoshiro Hayashi lent prestige as leaders of the committee. Prefectural and municipal participants in the initiative showed enthusiasm and provided significant tangible support.

---

[2]*Open Doors 1994–1995* reported Japan in first place among foreign countries with 45,280 students in U.S. higher education institutions (Institute of International Education, 1995).

Ambassadors of U.S. Higher Education

Only three U.S. branch campuses were realized as a direct result of this initiative, although the secretariat for the committee on the Japanese side estimated in 1988 that as many as 12 would be developed. All three—Southern Illinois University at Carbondale (SIUC)-Niigata (1988), Texas A&M-Koriyama (1990), and Minnesota State University-Akita (1990)—were U.S. public institutions linked with Japanese public entities (municipalities and their respective prefectures). The campuses opened with tremendous publicity.

Between 1988 and 1990 the number of branch campuses expanded quickly, the majority as partnerships with Japanese businessmen and not under the auspices of the U.S.-Japan Committee for Promoting Trade Expansion. Openings of branch campuses by privately sponsored partnerships received less attention than those involving public partnerships, where broad community interests were involved. Early closings, some ignoble and including one public partnership, had already begun by the time other campuses were just opening in 1990. Public and media attention surrounding later openings sometimes was filled with extreme reservation or skepticism. Fiscal irresponsibility and misrepresentation of programs in the case of some early closings, and student failures and dropouts in other continuing programs, contributed to a dramatic turn-around in the environment for U.S. branch campuses by the end of 1990.

From the beginning, the Japanese educational establishment had little enthusiasm for U.S. branch campuses. High school English teachers and others with an international outlook showed mild interest in the movement at first, but they were soon disenchanted as branch-campus students faced the realities of learning English and the consequences of failure in American-style higher education. Large numbers of students failed or dropped out. That the drop-out rate in Japanese higher education is very low in comparison with that in the United States was largely ignored or unknown by those who established branch campuses. This difference, along with apparent disregard for student welfare by some of the programs that closed, convinced many Japanese educators to advise students against attending a U.S. branch campus.

The attitude of high school teachers and administrators in Japan toward branch campuses was perhaps the single most important reason for gradually declining enrollments and many campus closings after 1990. In fact, probably few of them ever promoted branch campuses. As a group, high school teachers and administrators represent the status quo. Personal and school reputations rest on admission of students to the best Japanese colleges and universities.

Even where excellent relationships have existed locally between Japanese high schools and U.S. branch campuses, this attitude persists. English faculty at one of the surviving branch campuses, for instance, have contributed regularly on a formal contract basis to a special English curriculum at the local prefectural senior high school. Even there, however, teachers and administrators have told students to think of the high school's prestige and choose a Japanese university despite the students' desire to enroll at the branch campus.

At official government levels there has been limited recognition. In the cases of the two surviving branch campuses begun under the auspices of the U.S.-Japan Committee for Promoting Trade Expansion, the local and prefectural governments did award ad hoc recognition to them as colleges or universities. The Ministry of Education, however, has never recognized U.S. branch campuses. In fairness, apparently none have sought that recognition by means of application, although there have been continual complaints about the lack of recognition by many branch campuses. Obstacles related to infrastructure and fiscal stability undoubtedly are important reasons for not applying for recognition, but vague references to curricular issues are usually prominent in explanations by U.S. institutions as to why they have not applied. The Ministry's regulations concerning ownership of land, buildings, and equipment and the requirement of a sufficient endowment to preclude abrupt closures all, in fact, are related to academic standards. Further, the importance of infrastructure and fiscal stability to a sound academic program has been neglected by some U.S. branch campuses.

Efforts to Uphold Academic Standards
at Branch Campuses

From an early date there was concern about upholding academic standards at the branch campuses. Revelations about low academic standards at campuses that closed early, criticisms of campuses that offered U.S. credit for courses taught in Japanese by faculty with questionable academic credentials, and complaints about misrepresentation of the U.S. accreditation system stimulated such concern.

In a number of cases, the U.S. institutions failed to inform their regional accrediting associations of their plans and operations in Japan. One of the earliest serious expressions of concern was a visit in 1990 by then-Council on Postsecondary Accreditation (COPA) Vice President Marjorie Peace Lenn to Japan, at the invitation of the U.S. Embassy, to inform the Japanese public and authorities about U.S. higher education and the accreditation system. At a meeting for branch-campus leaders in the Tokyo American Center on that visit, she advised the erring ones to straighten up their operations.

The development and activities of the Association of American Colleges and Universities in Japan (AACUJ) merit recognition in regard to early efforts to uphold academic standards. Regular discussions began in 1989 among the Japan-based administrators of five U.S. branch-campus programs about the need for an organization.[3] The first meeting of what became the AACUJ was held in June 1990, at the U.S. Embassy in Tokyo, and semiannual meetings at various branch-campus sites were held after the U.S.-based association was organized officially in the winter of 1990–91. Guidelines were adopted in February 1991, and bylaws were approved in January 1992, in Dallas, Texas. Other forces influencing the development of the association were complex and included the U.S. institutions that formed the U.S. Foundation for International Economic Policy, members of the U.S. accreditation community who were becoming increasingly concerned about the branch-campus movement, and the U.S. Embassy in Tokyo, which reluctantly at first and more actively later encouraged and assisted the association.

Academic standards and control of them were of major importance to the early AACUJ because of growing criticisms of some branch-campus programs. Noting that it was not an accrediting agency, the AACUJ's guidelines stated that the organization's goal was to support academic quality. It limited its membership to accredited institutions that subscribed to the *Principles of Good Practice in Overseas International Education Programs for Non-U.S. Nationals.*[4] Courses offered by AACUJ members

---

[3]Participants in early discussions in Japan represented Tokyo International College, Los Angeles City College, the University of Nevada: Reno, Southern Illinois University at Carbondale-Niigata, and Temple University-Japan.
[4]Council on Postsecondary Accreditation (COPA), Regional Institutional Accrediting Bodies (Washington, D.C.: Council on Postsecondary Education, Regional Institutional Accrediting Bodies, 1990).

were to be "comparable" to those at the home institution and taught in English if so taught at the home campus. Furthermore, the U.S. institution was to maintain sole responsibility for the academic program at branches in Japan. Academic credentials of faculty were to be consistent with those of faculty at the home institution and all faculty personnel matters were to be the responsibility of the home campus or its formally designated chief academic officer in Japan.

The control issue was a somewhat divisive one for AACUJ members in the first year or two. A few institutions at which the Japanese partners wielded great overall authority desired an AACUJ with representation by both sides of the partnerships. At a November 1990 meeting in Washington, D.C., organized with the encouragement of COPA, a few Japanese partners attempted to participate and gain recognition in AACUJ. One such partner submitted a letter to that meeting stating that he had directed his American administrator in Japan to organize the AACUJ; thus, he took credit for the conception of the organization. The issue was settled at a meeting at the Tokyo American Cultural Center on February 7, 1992. Then-AACUJ President Charles B. Klasek clarified for all that the AACUJ was an association of U.S. institutions. Clearly not accepted within AACUJ, some Japanese partners then attempted to establish a counterpart organization. It failed to materialize.

While recruitment and other issues were part of the agenda in efforts at joint representation in AACUJ or a counterpart organization, the issue of control of academic affairs clearly also was involved. In 1991 AACUJ was launched with a membership of 20 institutions.[5] In June 1991 applications were invited for the role of providing secretariat services for AACUJ in Japan. Only the newly formed Laurasian Institution applied. This organization's founders included Philip Palin, an early and regular participant in pre-AACUJ discussions. The Laurasian Institution donated its services to AACUJ for a year, through spring 1992. This was the high

---

[5]The original AACUJ members were Arizona State University; Central Texas College; City University of New York-Herbert H. Lehman College; City University, Washington; Concordia College, Oregon; Edmonds Community College, Washington; Heidelberg College, Ohio; Los Angeles City College; McKendree College, Illinois; Minnesota State University System; Mount Hood Community College, Oregon; Oklahoma State University; Southern Illinois University at Carbondale; Sullivan County Community College, New York; Teachers' College-Columbia University; Temple University, Pennsylvania; Texas A&M University; University of Nevada: Reno; University of West Florida; and West Chester University of Pennsylvania.

point of the branch-campus movement and of the AACUJ. The Institution provided help with media relations (which were complicated and considerable at the time), conferencing, organizational development, and coordination with government and accrediting agencies. From September through April it actually published a monthly membership newsletter, *Ringsho*, and in December 1991, in cooperation with AACUJ, published a guidebook to U.S. higher education in Japan.[6] Both the newsletters and the book are valuable resources on the first year of AACUJ and its membership, and they document a zeal for upholding academic standards. The bilingual book focused on AACUJ members, with summaries of each, and included explanatory essays on U.S. higher education for the Japanese public. When the Laurasian Institution support for the secretariat ended on May 1, 1992, Lakeland College-Japan offered to house and staff the function of the secretariat on a much more limited basis. In the following years, branch campuses continued to close. As membership declined to the current seven full members and one associate and as media attention and interest in general in U.S. branch campuses declined, AACUJ and its secretariat's work changed and diminished significantly.

Declining membership in AACUJ was accompanied by fewer expressions of concern about academic standards and academic control. This was partly the result of the disappearance of many programs that had raised the concern; it was partly the result of the need to focus on basic survival issues. Recruitment and enrollment in a declining market were the major such issues after 1992. Interestingly, demographic facts about the declining college-age population in Japan had been known, but reasoned away, even as the explosion of programs began in 1987. Meanwhile, Japanese institutions expanded their own international programs and competed with branch campuses more vigorously and effectively in the declining market. And, the Japanese public became more aware and more daring regarding direct entry into higher education in the United States.

Since 1992 the recurring practical issues related to recruitment and enrollment, especially for branch campuses without status as educational institutions in Japan, have been student discounts on train passes,

---

[6]Laurasian Institution, *American Higher Education in Japan, 1992: A Guidebook for Students, Parents, and Teachers* (Laurasian Publications, 1992).

≈≈ In promoting their branch campuses and in making comparisons with Japanese higher education, U.S. institutions often mentioned academic quality and standards. The matter seemed to begin and end with the promotional material in a number of instances.

especially important for commuter schools, and visas for international students. Institutions with educational status as "specialty" schools (*Senshugakko*) have not encountered these problems to the same extent as those operating as for-profit corporations. Due to the latter, these problems remain issues for AACUJ, the U.S. Embassy, and the Japanese government.

In addition to efforts of the AACUJ, encouragement and assistance from COPA, and facilitation of efforts by the U.S. Embassy, the regional accrediting associations with oversight of programs in Japan have promoted the upholding of academic standards at the branch campuses. The North Central Association of Colleges and Schools, which had responsibility for the single greatest number of branches in Japan (eight at one time), showed particular concern and renewed its evaluation efforts by initiating three-year reviews of those programs under its accrediting jurisdiction in what it termed the "Japan Initiative." Considered as an experiment, the Japan Initiative called for teams of four members plus a North Central Association staffer to make site visits of approximately two days to each program under its jurisdiction every three years. A visit was to require an abbreviated self-study and a preparatory briefing of the team by a U.S.-based administrator of the site to be visited. Reports of an advisory and informational nature were to be prepared. The experiment was conducted only once in June 1994, when the SIUC, Heidelberg, and Huron University branch campuses were visited.[7] By 1994–95 the number of branch campuses in Japan had dwindled to fewer than a dozen altogether, and by the 1996 annual meeting of AACUJ in Chicago, only seven institutions had full membership.[8] A joint follow-up meeting of representatives from U.S. institutions and Japan-side U.S. administrators was held in February 1996 in Tokyo. Only two representatives came from the United States. It was decided then that annual meetings would take place in Japan rather than in the United States.

AACUJ now included only a handful of programs, the strengths and weaknesses of which were well known. The major concerns of the

[7]The visit to Huron University was a regular accreditation site visit, not part of the Japan Initiative.
[8]AACUJ members as of spring 1996 were Central Texas College (associate member); Edmonds Community College; Heidelberg College; Lakeland College, Wisconsin; Minnesota State University System; Southern Illinois University at Carbondale; Temple University; and Sullivan County Community College.

Ambassadors of U.S. Higher Education

members were by now practical affairs of survival. Loftier concerns such as upholding academic standards seemed to be matters for the individual institutions to address. At least the majority of the surviving AACUJ members in 1996 represented U.S. partners that maintained home-campus academic standards and U.S. control of academic affairs at branch campuses. They each had five or more years of history and most had begun to enjoy some degree of de facto recognition in Japan as college-level institutions. Any deficiencies in the programs of individual members were known and tolerated by the others.

Issues and Problems in Maintaining and Controlling Academic Standards at Branch Campuses

In promoting their branch campuses and in making comparisons with Japanese higher education, U.S. institutions often mentioned academic quality and standards. The matter seemed to begin and end with the promotional material in a number of instances. The actualities of contracts with Japanese partners and program operations in these cases hindered or prevented maintaining and controlling academic standards.

All the branch campuses opened as partnerships between U.S. institutions and Japanese interests, but the partnerships varied greatly regarding the goals for, and operation of, the campuses. In cases in which the considerable expenses of time, effort, and money needed to acquire knowledge and establish trust during contract negotiations were bearable to both sides, strong relationships developed and home-campus standards tended to survive low enrollments and various other problems. Even when such campuses closed, it was accomplished in an orderly fashion and with limited inconvenience to students and personnel. In cases in which the preliminary work was insufficient, academic standards tended to be disregarded and the results of closure were often calamitous. Whether or not related, low academic standards and problematic closings seemed to go hand in hand.

Stability is an important underpinning of academic quality, and one measure of the strength of programs has been the durability of the partnerships. Some branch campuses saw a need for changes in Japanese partners when difficulties arose. One branch campus experienced four or more partnership changes. Changes in partnerships all occurred in the private sector in which the Japanese partners were primarily businessmen. No such changes occurred in the public sector in which the

Japanese partners were municipalities and prefectures. Two of the remaining AACUJ member institutions broke with their partners in 1996 and expressed intentions to operate in 1996–97 without Japanese partners. This will be a significant development if it occurs.

At least to some extent, the legal status in Japan of U.S. branch campuses has hindered or fostered their respective academic programs and reputations. Those linked with municipalities and prefectures or with proprietors of established Japanese educational institutions generally sought and acquired legal status as educational institutions in Japan. The status has been either as "miscellaneous" schools (*Senmongakko*) or as "specialty" schools (*Senshugakko*). Sometimes miscellaneous status was granted for start-up purposes while applications were being processed for specialty status. While this kind of recognition was not equal to the college status granted by the Ministry of Education, the specialty school designation did bring benefits in the forms of rail pass discounts for students, foreign student visas, and the possibility of financial subsidies from municipal and prefectural governments. Branch campuses that did not acquire school status of any sort remained for-profit corporations without such benefits.

The relationship between physical infrastructure and academic standards seems to have been almost totally ignored by a few branch campuses and treated very lightly by others. Most of these never reached the point of delivering academic credit courses and ultimately closed. They tended to be partnerships with Japanese businessmen whose resources were based on real estate ventures that eventually suffered after the bursting of the bubble economy. In some cases, space on a few floors of a building or even parts of floors in several different buildings were utilized for classrooms and administrative offices. Infrastructure for these programs amounted to desks or tables and chairs in a few rooms, a few portable chalkboards, a few computers, and perhaps a library amounting to a bookshelf of used books. This description even applied to two or three programs in which credit-bearing courses were offered in the early years.

Operational funds for direct support of the branch campus—for teaching materials, equipment, faculty development, etc.—also were often controlled by the Japanese partner. The implications for academic standards should enrollment decline or should the partner encounter economic hardship were not foreseen in such contract arrangements. In one case of a U.S. two-year public college linked with a private Japanese businessman, the U.S. administrator claimed that this was the perfect arrangement. According to him, the relationship was so strong and the Japanese partner such a committed benefactor that everything needed would be provided. Other branch campus administrators observed that his campus facilities suggested the program needs were slight indeed. They amounted to nothing more than described earlier. The committed benefactor later withdrew support quite suddenly when his economic bubble burst and the campus closed after a few months' notice.

Maintenance and control of academic standards in a program begin with recruitment and other public relations efforts. Contracts between the partners generally called for the U.S. side to approve students for admission, but in cases where the Japanese partner exerted control or filled a void left by the U.S. partner, such approval was generally inadequate. The quality of students attracted to the programs eventually affected academic standards. Furthermore, especially in some early problem cases, misrepresentation of accreditation status, quality of faculty or facilities, credit transferability, and prospects for student progress at the branch campus contributed to public mistrust and threat of legal action by aggrieved students. In at least one troublesome case of misrepresentation, the U.S. partners assumed that the Japanese side knew the market and showed undue trust in a newly formed relationship. In others, honest misinterpretation or inadequate bilingual skills were to blame.

Admission qualifications and academic promotion of students also influenced academic standards at some branch campuses. Pressures to lower standards were both direct and indirect. Whether or not home-campus admission standards were enforced at all was questioned in more than one instance. Some U.S. administrators complained in the early years about Japanese partners who applied pressure without reservation. Another problem arose when control of admission and records was totally in the hands of the Japanese side of the partnership. At times the U.S. side was even unaware of the basic operations. In the case of one comprehensive public university linked with a Japanese business partner, student records were under the control of the Japanese partner through the time of the closing, and the U.S. side admitted it was unable even to communicate directly with students about the closing because it lacked access to the student records.

≋ *When the provost's office was involved, the necessary attention was usually given to maintaining academic standards.*

Undoubtedly indirect pressures affected academic standards in subtle ways at many branch campuses. For example, financial shortages and low enrollments may affect attitudes about admitting and promoting students without direct pressure from partners. Also, faculty relations with the Japanese community at large may gradually alter U.S. attitudes about academic standards. Furthermore, the nature of the classroom situation in which a U.S. college teacher faces a dominant non-U.S. culture probably has a natural impact on teaching methodology and evaluation. Awareness of such problems and consistent efforts to maintain home-campus standards have been encouraged by a strong U.S. position in the overall operation of some branch campuses.

Other U.S. institutions simply delivered courses and supplied teachers, with minimal administrative supervision or support at the branch campus. Where this was the extent of the involvement in a branch campus, the risks to maintaining home-campus standards were greater.

Personnel policies at branch campuses are also related to maintaining home-campus standards. Sometimes personnel contracts were handled by the Japanese partner. The dangers there were clear. Maintaining and controlling standards were also difficult when administrators and faculty were recruited primarily or entirely from outside the home institution. At branches at which standards were questioned and criticized most seriously, administrators and faculty tended to be recruited from outside. Sometimes there was no more than an interview at the home campus for even the administrators of the branch campus. In at least one private college initiative, there was not even an interview. On the other hand, U.S. institutions that achieved recognition for branch programs of good quality tended to recruit both administrators and significant numbers of faculty from the home campus for at least the credit-bearing parts of their branch-campus programs. The value of complete familiarity with home-campus standards and strong home-campus ties and support was proved in these latter cases.

Finally, the positioning of the branch campus in the home-campus administrative structure is also related to concern for academic standards at the branch campuses. When the provost's office was involved, the necessary attention was usually given to maintaining academic standards. This was also the case in the few instances where the president's or chancellor's office had oversight of the program. In at least two instances in which an international program office at the home campus had oversight, academic standards were seriously questioned by administrators at other branch campuses.

SIUC-N: A Success Story

The SIUC (Southern Illinois University at Carbondale) branch campus in Niigata (SIUC-N) was established in May 1988, in response to the initiative of the U.S.-Japan Committee for Promoting Trade Expansion to attract U.S. academic programs to Japan. SIUC became the lead institution for the Mid-America State Universities Association (renamed the Association of Big Eight Universities in 1989) in its response to the initiative. The agreement between SIUC and Nakajo Town in Niigata Prefecture placed full authority and responsibility for all academic and many support services with SIUC. It became a model for the matching of an American comprehensive public university with a Japanese municipality in the establishment of a branch campus with a distinctively American character.

As the first branch campus to open under the initiative, SIUC-N enjoyed extensive favorable attention. Nakajo Town, its host, held great expectations. U.S. flags and welcome signs of all sorts adorned practically every shop and lamppost. Citizens of all ages and occupations studied English in preparation for the influx of U.S. teachers. Admitted students and their parents saw it as an excellent educational opportunity; some saw it as redemption from the Japanese education system. Town and prefecture envisioned it as a vehicle for cultural, social, and economic enhancement. The media gave daily and generally supportive coverage estimated to be worth millions of dollars in the months prior to the opening of the campus.

From the outset, SIUC saw exciting potential in the branch-campus initiative. For much of the previous decade, SIUC had explored possibilities for expanding opportunities in Japan for its faculty and students. For several decades, SIUC had maintained a sizable Japanese student enrollment in its undergraduate and graduate programs, had developed exchange opportunities for faculty and students at Japanese institutions, and had expanded Japanese language and cultural course offerings. The establishment of a branch campus in Japan offered a significantly greater expansion of opportunities, however, than any previous activity. In developing its response to the initiative, SIUC placed priority on long-range and rather intangible and nonspecific benefits.

The SIUC-N academic program replicates home-campus programs and has two parts: credit-free intensive English-language instruction and credit-bearing courses equivalent to the freshman and sophomore years of an SIUC bachelor's degree program (referred to here as the Core Curriculum). Also, a one-year, credit-bearing Japanese language and culture program is offered at SIUC-N for students from the home campus and other U.S. colleges and universities. All elements of the SIUC-N academic program are tied closely to the home campus in terms of content and standards.

Students who are admitted to SIUC-N must demonstrate English proficiency before enrolling in credit courses. Students with a TOEFL score of 520 or higher may enroll directly in the Core Curriculum, and a small number of students has been admitted in this way each year since 1989. For admission to SIUC-N, applicants must pass an entrance examination composed of English-language and Japanese-essay sections and have a high school grade-point average of 3.00 on a 5.00 scale. Admission procedures are entirely controlled by SIUC. An SIUC admission officer is a member of the SIUC-N administration in Nakajo. A direct computer link to the home campus allows the SIUC-N admission officer and other administrators to perform their functions as if they were located in Carbondale.

In terms of administrative, teaching, and support personnel, SIUC-N also is tied closely to the home campus. The director, who holds the title Principal because of the legal status of the branch campus as a specialty school, is a long-term administrator from the home campus and has served as director of SIUC-N since its inception. The faculty members who teach intensive English are appointed by the home campus. They hold at least an M.A. in teaching English as a Second Language and have had a minimum of three years' experience. Approximately one-half have had previous experience at the home campus as faculty members or graduate students. Faculty in the Core Curriculum are a mixture of members of departments at the home campus who rotate to Nakajo for a semester and faculty with longer-term commitments to the branch campus. The SIUC-N calendar coincides exactly with that of the home campus to facilitate faculty, staff, and student movement.

Ambassadors of U.S. Higher Education

The intensive English-language component is based on the program offered at the home campus in the Center for English as a Second Language (CESL) and is administered by the Linguistics Department in the College of Liberal Arts. In this component, students have 20 hours of classroom instruction per week (reading, writing, grammar, speaking, and listening), plus language and computer laboratories. Instruction is offered at eight levels during five 9-week terms every 12 months. Institutional TOEFL scores determine placement level on entrance. The Core Curriculum courses at Nakajo are carefully monitored by home-campus departments, and textbooks and syllabi are determined there. To an extent impossible at the home campus, out-of-class support is provided at the same time that standards are maintained.

SIUC-N reached its highest enrollment of 630 full-time students in 1990 and has experienced a yearly decline since to the 1995–96 figure of 325. Students have been almost evenly divided between intensive English and Core Curriculum studies since 1990. As of January 1996, a total of 554 students had completed the SIUC-N program and transferred to the home campus or to other U.S. colleges and universities as juniors. Since 1989, when the first credit-bearing courses were introduced, over 39,000 semester credit hours have been generated at SIUC-N and logged on home-campus transcripts.

A tracking system for transfer students was implemented at the home campus when the program started, and the academic success of transfer students has been notable. Three hundred students had completed undergraduate degrees as of fall 1995, many with academic honors. Several have completed graduate degrees and several dozen are engaged in graduate studies in the United States or Japan. Grade-point averages at the home campus remained approximately the same as at SIUC-N for over 90 percent of the transfer students, and there have been only a few academic suspensions of transfer students at the home campus since 1989. SIUC administrators and faculty members have regularly expressed satisfaction with the academic performance of SIUC-N students.

Future Prospects for U.S. Branch Campuses in Japan

The phenomenon of U.S. branch campuses in Japan was characterized by a spectacular beginning and early growth followed by a sudden reversal and decline over several years. Many early doubts were

≋ The level of commitment of U.S. institutions involved in branch campuses in Japan to academic standards of high quality has been reflected in their willingness to adequately finance the endeavors.

expressed about the ability of such programs to survive and about the potential for maintaining high U.S. academic standards in the context of complex interests and forces. The doubts were well-founded, as the history of the branch campuses has indicated. Only a handful of branch campuses remain, and there have been many instances in which branch campuses have failed to maintain high academic standards.

The factors contributing to maintaining and controlling academic standards suggested by the experiences of branch campuses in Japan have financial implications. The establishment of strong and stable partnerships, legal educational status, appropriate infrastructure, home-campus control of guaranteed operational funds, and comparable admission procedures and personnel is labor intensive. The level of commitment of U.S. institutions involved in branch campuses in Japan to academic standards of high quality has been reflected in their willingness to adequately finance the endeavors.

It seems reasonable to assume that at least several small-sized branch campuses will continue to survive and maintain the academic standards of their respective home institutions. The enrollment pool is adequate if judged by Japanese interest in U.S. higher education. And, especially in cases where broad public interests are served, financial resources appear to be sufficient. The survivors can continue to maintain high academic standards if they remain ever diligent with respect to issues of program quality and control.

Dr. Jared H. Dorn is director/principal of the Southern Illinois University at Carbondale in Niigata campus, and has served in that capacity since its opening. He previously directed the International Programs of SIUC, and has taught in or administered university programs in Taiwan, Jordan, and the West Bank. His writing has covered a broad range of educational topics.

CHAPTER 6

Case Study: A Twinning Program in Malaysia: Lessons from the Field

Charles Reafsnyder
Associate Dean, International Research and Development
Indiana University, Bloomington, Indiana

Introduction

Offshore academic programs can improve the educational quality of institutions in the United States and abroad. For U.S. educators, overseas academic programs offer opportunities to broaden teaching and research experiences, assist in the recruitment of new students, and forge strategic linkages with government agencies and private corporations abroad. For the overseas counterpart, such programs satisfy unmet educational needs and contribute to institution-building in the host country through faculty and curriculum development and the transfer of valuable research skills and technology. In recent years, Malaysia has sought these benefits through "twinning arrangements" with overseas institutions. In a twinning arrangement, an overseas institution provides one or two years' instruction in the host country; thereafter, students transfer abroad to the home institution to complete their degree programs.

In Malaysia, twinning programs are a growth industry. At a key intersection in Kuala Lumpur, an enormous billboard advertises a local private college as a "pioneer" in twinning programs and lists six institutions, three from the United States and three from the United Kingdom and Australia, as its partners. Evening radio advertisements regularly promote external degree programs from Australia, and Sunday newspapers are full of ads and articles about new, for-profit institutions of higher education promising students "significant savings" while earning "advanced credit" toward degrees at overseas institutions. In addition to a burgeoning number of private twinning programs, the government of Malaysia recently announced plans for five large government-owned corporations to establish their own diploma- and degree-granting institutions. In response, each of these companies established relationships with overseas "twinning" partners.

≋ *These programs are extraordinarily complex to manage in a way that delivers quality education comparable to what is offered at the home institution. Yet, that is what students, parents, and official sponsors abroad expect to receive in return for their investment of time and money.*

While the benefits of such programs are attractive to many overseas institutions, these programs are extraordinarily complex to manage in a way that delivers quality education comparable to what is offered at the home institution. Yet, that is what students, parents, and official sponsors abroad expect to receive in return for their investment of time and money. The challenges faced in offering such programs abroad range from inadequate funding, differing institutional structures and traditions, shortages of qualified faculty, language and cultural barriers (for faculty as well as students), and unpredictable enrollments to complex laws, regulations, and political considerations in the host country. In new environments, many traditional practices of the home institution must be adapted and modified for a new and collaborative educational program abroad to succeed.

This case study focuses on a U.S. program offering instruction abroad to host country nationals, and describes the experience of a Malaysian twinning program in which government-sponsored students received two years of instruction from faculty approved and appointed by Indiana University. Course work completed by students in the program was validated on an Indiana University transcript. The program was conducted under the auspices of the Midwest Universities Consortium for International Activities, Inc. (MUCIA), of which Indiana University is a member, and the Institut Teknologi MARA (ITM) in Shah Alam, Malaysia, on behalf of the Malaysian Department of Public Services and the Malaysian Ministry of Education.

Historical Background
To understand the rationale and mission of the program in its Malaysian context, it is first necessary to examine the historical situation that produced the need for the program. Following Malaysian independence in 1957 Bumiputra (ethnic Malays and other indigenous peoples), who made up slightly more than half of Malaysia's population, were underrepresented in business and the professions. As a group, they had a per capita average income barely half that of other ethnic groups in Malaysia and owned only 2 percent of the corporate equity in the country. To promote social equality and political stability, the government of Malaysia instituted an affirmative action program in the 1970s, "The New Economic Plan (NEP)," designed to advance Bumiputra

Ambassadors of U.S. Higher Education

educational attainment and technical skills. The NEP also aimed to develop a larger skilled labor force to attract foreign investment and diminish reliance on foreign technical expertise. The goal was to raise personal income and increase Bumiputra ownership in Malaysian corporate equity to 30 percent. In the 1980s, industrialization and foreign investment produced an accompanying demand for skilled workers. The mission of the Institut Teknologi MARA, as an affirmative action educational program, was to address these needs by providing postsecondary education to increasing numbers of Bumiputra.

In addition, the NEP provided large numbers of scholarships for overseas study to Bumiputra. Students were sent abroad in part because local universities could not expand their capacity fast enough to meet the country's manpower needs. As a result, in 1984 more than 14,000 government-sponsored students were enrolled in degree programs in the United States; similar numbers were enrolled in the United Kingdom. In both countries, two problems became the focus of attention:

- Many students from rural areas were not making a successful academic transition at overseas institutions; and

- Maintaining large numbers of sponsored students abroad was costly for the Malaysian government.

In 1985 the government proposed addressing these problems through the establishment of a U.S.-style program that would provide the first two years of instruction in Malaysia. The government hoped that the program would accomplish four objectives:

1. Reduce first-year failure rates, enabling students to become familiar with U.S. standards and curricula without having to make a simultaneous social and cultural adjustment.

2. Reduce the cost of instruction for the first two years of undergraduate study compared to the cost of study in the United States.

3. Increase the number of government-sponsored students attending high-quality institutions in the United States.

≋ *The Program had a secure funding source, a guaranteed supply of under-graduate students from a country in which English is widely spoken, a physical facility in Shah Alam suitable for the purpose, and an attractive package of salary, benefits, and allowances.*

4. Distribute student placements among different regions and institutions in the United States to avoid large Malaysian student concentrations that would impede language acquisition and social adjustment.

The ITM/MUCIA Cooperative Program

In 1984 Indiana University (IU) was approached by officials of the Malaysian government about the possibility of setting up a two-year program in Malaysia with IU courses and credits. Because of the size and financial complexity of the project, IU decided to approach MUCIA to serve as the prime contractor for the project. IU would serve as subcontractor and "lead institution" for MUCIA in the program; IU and the other MUCIA member institutions would provide faculty.[1] ITM was designated by the Malaysian Ministry of Education to provide facilities and support for the program. Based in Shah Alam, Malaysia, the ITM/MUCIA Cooperative Program was funded by the Malaysian government and accepted its first students in June 1985.

The program provided two years of IU course work to students preparing for U.S. bachelor's degree programs in engineering, business, and computer science. Between 1,200 and 1,500 students took courses at the ITM/MUCIA Center each year. After 10 years of cooperative effort, in 1995 Indiana University transferred academic control of the program to ITM. By then, more than 4,500 Malaysian students had completed the two-year program and transferred into upper-division programs in the United States.

As a twinning program, the ITM/MUCIA Cooperative Program operated under almost ideal circumstances. It had a secure funding source, a guaranteed supply of undergraduate students from a country in which English is widely spoken, a physical facility in Shah Alam suitable for the purpose, and an attractive package of salary, benefits, and allowances with which to recruit experienced U.S. faculty. In addition, the program provided funding for an administrative unit at IU to handle faculty recruitment and orientation, maintenance of student records, monitoring of student academic performance, and placement. Moreover, the host institution, the Institut Teknologi MARA, was well-recognized in

---

[1]In 1985 the MUCIA member institutions included the University of Minnesota, the University of Illinois, Indiana University, the University of Iowa, Michigan State University, Ohio State University, Purdue University, and the University of Wisconsin–Madison. Subsequently, the University of Michigan and Pennsylvania State University joined the consortium.

Ambassadors of U.S. Higher Education

the United States and had ample means to support the program. Finally, while the U.S. participants had never operated a twinning program before, both Indiana University and MUCIA had extensive experience in the management of other kinds of overseas training and educational programs.

The host-country sponsor and MUCIA shared concerns about academic quality because government-sponsored students had to perform successfully in upper-division programs throughout the United States. The government hoped that the students would receive enough transfer credit for their course work in Malaysia to be able to complete their studies in the United States in two or two-and-a-half years. Given the general acceptability of Indiana University transfer credits, the prospects for achieving this latter objective were good.

Program Outcomes

Measured in terms of output, the ITM/MUCIA Cooperative Program was successful in meeting its objectives and in sustaining a quality offshore academic program during the 10 years of its operation. These output measures included the following:

- ITM/MUCIA students were accepted at over 160 U.S. universities with a credit transfer rate of better than 95 percent;

- Students' grade-point averages (GPA) at these universities *improved* from an average 2.65 GPA (on a 4-point scale) at the ITM/MUCIA Center to a combined 2.79 GPA in the United States as they transferred from the program in Malaysia to upper-division programs in the United States;

- All but a small number of students completed their bachelor's degree programs in two to two-and-a-half years of study after matriculation from the ITM/MUCIA program; and

- The percentage of Malaysian students matriculating to U.S. universities ranked as "very competitive" or higher (according to *Barron's Profiles of American Colleges*) doubled during the life of the program compared with the placement of government-sponsored students in the years before the ITM/MUCIA program. By 1991 more than 90 percent of the students were matriculating to universities ranked very competitive or higher.

In addition, the program shortened the stay abroad of Malaysian students and reduced the cost of the first two years of instruction. Although IU and MUCIA did not have access to a full accounting of ITM's support costs in Shah Alam, estimates of ITM's costs added to MUCIA's expenditures showed a cost per student, per year in Shah Alam that resulted in savings of 40–50 percent over the cost of sending students directly to the United States. Initially, the program's savings were much smaller, but they increased as economies of scale and the replacement of U.S. faculty with Malaysian instructors reduced overall costs.

To achieve this success, the program had to adapt the quality assurance measures traditional at U.S. institutions to the offshore program's setting and objectives. The following discussion describes the development and organization of the ITM/MUCIA program as well as some of the adaptations that were made during this 10-year experience in cooperative international education.

Program Mission and Objectives
A key question in any collaborative offshore program is: What are the goals and objectives of the participating institutions? For their part, IU and MUCIA defined the following major objectives of their participation in the program:

1. Establish a program that would be conducted in accordance with established academic standards and principles consistent with those in effect at the lead institution, Indiana University.

2. Build the capacity of the Malaysian faculty and staff to conduct the program on their own so that it could continue successfully, later on, under ITM auspices.

3. Through teaching assignments in Malaysia, "internationalize" MUCIA faculty, especially in the arts and sciences where there are typically few long-term overseas teaching opportunities.

Ambassadors of U.S. Higher Education

4. Build the capacity of member institutions to manage and conduct overseas programs.

5. Provide an external source of income to MUCIA and its participating universities.

In one way or another, these objectives guided virtually all major decisions by MUCIA concerning the program.

Quality Assurance Standards for the Offshore Program

In the ITM/MUCIA program, IU sought to employ the same procedures and standards for academic administration, admission, faculty hiring, curriculum development, instruction, and recordkeeping that were in effect at IU's home campuses. While the *Principles of Good Practices in Overseas International Education Programs for Non-U.S. Nationals*, described elsewhere in this book, were not available at the time the program began, the practices employed in the program anticipated these standards in most respects. In general, IU was guided in developing the design of the program by the standards applied by its regional accrediting agency to other IU off-campus academic programs.

To ensure that it had sufficient academic control over the program to warrant providing an IU transcript for work completed in it, IU secured agreement with all participating parties on the following principles of operation:

• The twinning program's academic "home" would be an academic unit at IU.
  This meant that academic policy, procedures, and standards would be established by the academic unit at IU responsible for authorizing the issuance of university credit. During the first half of the program, this unit was the IU School of Continuing Studies; during the latter half, it was the Undergraduate Education Center on the campus of Indiana University–Purdue University Indianapolis (IUPUI). Admission standards, plans of study, academic probation and dismissal policies, and the awarding of associate degrees were determined by the appropriate academic administrator in these supervising units. None of these policies were determined by nonfaculty or nonacademic administrative units.

≋ *In general, IU was guided in developing the design of the program by the standards applied by its regional accrediting agency to other IU off-campus academic programs.*

- Courses and syllabi for the programs of study offered in Malaysia would be supervised by specific, individual departments in the IU system.[2]
A department liaison (faculty member) drafted syllabi, laboratory manuals, and technical laboratory requirements that were required to be the same as those in effect in the supervising IU department. These were formally approved by the department chair. Any changes in syllabi (including texts) proposed by the teaching faculty in Malaysia also required approval from the chairperson of the sponsoring department. The syllabi addressed such things as required texts, objectives, weekly schedules of topics and readings, and recommendations for grading, standards, and assignments. Faculty in Shah Alam were expected to make up their own examinations and to supplement the syllabi and texts with materials of their own choosing.

- Faculty appointments would require department approvals.
Neither the provost of the ITM/MUCIA program, his Malaysian counterpart, nor the administrative staff at IU had authority to appoint faculty to the program. The department liaison supervising the course or courses that the faculty member was to teach reviewed each and every applicant's file and ranked candidates for each position. Faculty approvals and appointments were made for specific courses, not necessarily for all courses offered in the subject at Shah Alam. For example, electrical engineering faculty were not approved to teach mechanical engineering courses unless they had demonstrated knowledge of the latter at their home institution.
The minimum requirement for appointment was a master's degree in the appropriate discipline and two years of university-level teaching experience. The preferred credential was a Ph.D. and a continuing appointment at a recognized institution of higher education. While the ITM/MUCIA contract did not initially anticipate hiring Malaysian instructors for the IU program, subsequent circumstances led to the gradual addition of Malaysians to the center's teaching faculty. When this occurred, the review and appointment of Malaysian candidates

---

[2]The majority of the participating departments were from either the IU-Bloomington campus or Indiana University-Purdue University Indianapolis. One course (in political science) was supervised by the relevant department at the campus of Indiana University-Purdue University, Fort Wayne.

Ambassadors of U.S. Higher Education

proposed by the Institut Teknologi MARA were conducted in the same way as for expatriate faculty.

- Admission standards and student recordkeeping would be the same as at the responsible home academic unit and campus.

Admission requirements for the twinning program were the same as for Malaysian and other international students applying for freshman admission at IU's main campus. Students who met other minimum admission requirements but whose English was not yet sufficient for university-level study entered an intensive English-as-a-Second-Language program and continued in it until they had achieved sufficient mastery to undertake university-level course work. Students who were admitted were assigned IU student numbers and entered into the IU student records system at the home campus along with all other IU students. Their academic records were maintained at IU, and grade reports and transcripts were issued by IU for their course work in Malaysia at the end of each semester.

- Faculty governance would operate in accordance with the policies in effect at Indiana University as well as the specific requirements of the program.

Faculty at the ITM/MUCIA Center were appointed by the IU board of trustees as visiting faculty of Indiana University on fixed-term appointments. As such, they were subject to the terms of their individual contracts, the general agreement between ITM and MUCIA, and the academic policies of Indiana University. Faculty appointments were one-year teaching contracts that were renewable subject to evaluation by the provost of the ITM/MUCIA Center. The provost, appointed by IU and approved by the MUCIA board, reported to the dean of the supervising academic unit at IU on academic matters and to the president's office at IU and the MUCIA board of directors regarding contractual and administrative issues. As chief academic officer, the provost was charged with supervising the work of MUCIA faculty and staff on-site in Malaysia to ensure that contractual teaching obligations were met, quality assurance standards were observed, and unanticipated academic program needs were addressed. In Malaysia, the faculty were organized into disciplinary groups headed by an area coordinator. Area coordinators were responsible for scheduling, evaluating the need for curricular revision, tracking student progress, class assignments, department examinations, and other academic matters. Final authority over courses in Shah Alam, however, remained with the academic departments at IU. A council of academic deans at IU provided guidance on broad policy matters related to the academic program.

- Evaluation of the program would include regular monitoring of output measures (e.g., grade-point averages, transfer credit awards, graduation rates) and periodic review by external examiners.

Consultants were hired from NAFSA: Association of International Educators and IU's own School of Education to evaluate the feasibility and merits of the proposed program, and comments on the program's design were solicited from the North Central Association of Colleges and Schools. In addition, MUCIA funded from its own sources visits of admission officers from each of the MUCIA schools, two program reviews from the MUCIA Project Review Committee (composed of board members from other MUCIA schools), and frequent visits from other MUCIA board members to obtain independent evaluations of the program. MUCIA project staff at IU made regular presentations about the program at national meetings of higher education associations, and course syllabi and program descriptions were published and distributed to every institution in the United States receiving the program's transfer students. In Malaysia, the program maintained regular communication and liaison with the Malaysian-American Commission on Educational Exchange. Finally, when the Undergraduate Education Center at IUPUI, the supervising academic unit, took part in IUPUI's 10-year accreditation self-study and review for the North Central Association of Colleges and Schools, the ITM/MUCIA program self-study was included in the report and the results were published.

Sufficient staffing was guaranteed in the initial agreement with the government of Malaysia to permit regular evaluation of student academic performance. As a result, throughout the program MUCIA project staff at IU produced regular reports for the provost, IU academic units, and Malaysian counterparts on such things as grades, transfer credits, length of time to complete the two-year program, teaching loads, length of time to complete the bachelor's degree, and academic dismissal rates.

Effectiveness of Quality Assurance Standards

All the quality assurance standards described above were implemented as planned. Academic deans and departments at IU cooperated to an exceptional degree in administering the offshore program. To the extent to which Malaysian counterparts, MUCIA faculty in Shah Alam, or the MUCIA board and executive office requested flexibility, the responsible home-campus academic units showed a willingness to adapt when convinced that doing so would not detract from the academic rigor of the program. This close supervision of the curriculum ensured that IU departments knew and vouched for what was being taught in their courses in Malaysia. Moreover, given the frequent turnover of MUCIA faculty in Shah Alam, continuity in the curriculum was ensured.

Procedures for the appointment of faculty also generally worked well. Candidates were initially interviewed by the administrative staff at IU, and referees were contacted by phone. As noted previously, the applications of candidates were then reviewed by both the supervising academic department at IU and the provost in Malaysia. Each set of reviewers rank-ordered the candidates in terms of preference. If the program staff in Malaysia or at IU preferred a candidate other than the one ranked highest by the supervising academic department, a specific request had to be made to the department in order to appoint that candidate. This careful selection process generally resulted in an experienced faculty; the great majority of faculty appointed to the program were tenured associate or full professors.[3]

Because of a nationwide shortage of Malaysian candidates for university faculty positions, however, Malaysians with Ph.D. degrees were rarely available. When circumstances (described below) necessitated the addition of increasing numbers of Malaysian instructors to the teaching staff, a system for training local master's degree holders to assume teaching positions had to be developed. At the suggestion of Malaysian counterparts, a training program designed by the IU math coordinator

[3]Throughout most of the program's operation, the breakdown of expatriate faculty by rank at the home institution was as follows: full professor (35 percent), associate professor (30 percent), assistant professor (20 percent), and instructor (15 percent). Seventy-six percent of the faculty were tenured at a U.S. institution and 60 percent were from MUCIA campuses.

in Bloomington became a model for other disciplines. In this model, individuals with an M.A. degree and no prior teaching experience began as "associate instructors" who assisted the regular faculty in instructional tasks. Much as with graduate students in U.S. doctoral programs, associate instructors were given occasional opportunities to teach under supervision. As they gained experience and demonstrated mastery of the subject matter, their supervised responsibilities were expanded to include more frequent teaching opportunities, preparation of tests, etc. After approximately two years of supervised teaching and with the recommendation of the area coordinator and faculty supervisor in Shah Alam, as well as the approval of the IU department liaison, such faculty could be promoted to "instructor of record" with full authority to teach the course or courses for which they had received specific approval. In the case of the mathematics department in Malaysia, which had the largest number of associate instructors, the IU math department liaison traveled to Malaysia to observe classes as part of the evaluation process. In addition, a limited number of senior-level and first-year graduate courses in mathematics were offered by MUCIA for credit on site to associate instructors as math refreshers. In other disciplines, faculty offered short-term seminars and workshops to prospective instructors.

Experienced Faculty as an Antidote to Short-Term Contracts

Some of the quality assurance standards that exist on a home campus cannot be fully replicated in twinning programs, e.g., the tenure process for the review, evaluation, and appointment of faculty was never part of the ITM/MUCIA program. Rather, selection favored expatriate faculty from MUCIA universities who were already tenured at their home institution.

Most expatriate faculty (excluding ESL instructors) stayed for only one or two years. This was the case for two interrelated reasons. First, most MUCIA faculty could only secure leaves of absence for one or two years. Indeed, one of MUCIA's objectives in the program was to internationalize MUCIA faculty so that they could share what they learned abroad with their home campuses upon return to the United States. Second, initial discussions about the program predicted a five-year life span for it. There was thus no stated intention initially on the Malaysian side to create a permanent program in Shah Alam with an expatriate faculty. The program was seen as an expedient until local institutions could absorb more students. After the program had been in operation for two years, the idea of an ITM-administered program staffed with local faculty began to be articulated as a future objective. The need to include increasing numbers of Malaysian faculty on the center's teaching staff was an additional factor limiting the desirability of long-term contracts for expatriate faculty.

In point of fact, short-term contracts are the rule in twinning programs rather than the exception. Administrators in such programs usually do not want to make long-term commitments to faculty in the face of uncertain enrollments; this is especially true where twinning programs operate on a for-profit basis. Short-term contracts make it possible to adjust more easily to shifting enrollments and to replace unproductive faculty, when necessary. Where government-financed programs exist, political and fiscal considerations typically dictate that expatriate faculty will only fill a short-term need until a larger pool of local faculty becomes available.

Short-term contracts, however, also make it more difficult to retain good faculty and to influence the performance of faculty during comparatively brief residences abroad. The high rate of turnover in faculty (approximately 40 percent per year for expatriate faculty) in the IU program limited the effectiveness of peer reviews. Likewise, promotion, tenure, and merit increases in salary, by which academic administrators motivate improved professional performance, mean relatively little to expatriate faculty who anticipate being involved in the program for only 12 to 24 months and who have a secure position to which to return. For their part, the home departments from which the faculty come often express little interest in faculty performance overseas. Only two or three times, from among the more than 300 expatriate faculty who served between 1985–95, did departments request appraisals of faculty performance in Shah Alam. Indeed, some faculty were penalized by their home institutions with below-average raises during their involvement in the overseas program. Had more home departments valued faculty participation in the international program and rewarded good performance, some of the effects of short-term employment in the program would have been ameliorated.

In addition, the resources that promote faculty and staff development at home may not be available in twinning programs. Research libraries, professional seminars and colloquia, teaching resource centers, staff

≈≈≈ Operation of such a complex project provides numerous examples of gray areas, unanswered questions, and problems that must be addressed by everyone at the same time.

training programs, and research facilities simply may not exist. Where they do, they may not be accessible to visiting faculty members. Given the negative effect of short-term contracts on traditional methods of professional evaluation and development, the ITM/MUCIA program found it imperative to hire a majority of the faculty from continuing appointments at recognized colleges and universities. Since the program offered the initial two years of undergraduate education, recruitment focused on candidates with especially good teaching credentials.

MUCIA took measures to ensure that a sufficient number of well-qualified faculty would be recruited for the program. Principally, these took the form of a compensation package that provided for salary and benefits at home-institution rates and sufficient additional allowances to ensure that individuals and two-income families did not lose financially by virtue of teaching in the program. In addition, the active participation of MUCIA ensured support from administrators for recruiting faculty from the eight main MUCIA campuses as well as from 29 other branch or regional campuses. In all, faculty were recruited from more than 40 U.S. universities, and the vast majority of them performed conscientiously and well.

Program Challenges and Adaptations
While it is comparatively easy to describe the overall mission and objectives of an overseas program, the day-to-day operation of such a complex project provides numerous examples of gray areas, unanswered questions, and problems that must be addressed by everyone at the same time. The following discussion focuses on some of the problems that confronted Malaysian and U.S. administrators in planning and implementing the ITM/MUCIA program. These could not have been overcome without cooperation, flexibility, and often a sense of humor on the part of all administrators involved.

Differing Philosophies of Education
The Institut Teknologi MARA is a diploma-granting institution that was initially created in the late 1960s as a rural development institute. Heavily influenced by the British model of higher education, ITM's curriculum focused on the delivery of technical skills through predetermined course sequences. At ITM proper and in the ITM/MUCIA program, students were obligated under the terms of their scholarships

to study a specific field of study and to complete the bachelor's degree within a limited period of time. At the end of the program, students would advance into upper-division U.S. programs in engineering, computer science, and business from which they would graduate within two years of their arrival in the United States. From the government's perspective, the objective of the program was to move students as quickly as possible through the curriculum to satisfy the private sector demand for skilled labor. Thus, many ITM administrators approached the twinning program as a technical training exercise.

This view clashed with the liberal arts tradition in U.S. higher education. The battleground for this clash of educational philosophies was the broad-based curriculum of the Associate of General Studies (A.G.S.) degree offered by the IU School of Continuing Studies. Based on a belief that problem-solving skills and creativity are enhanced by exposure to multiple disciplines, IU academic planners instituted A.G.S. degree requirements, which included a healthy dose of the humanities and social sciences along with mathematics and the physical sciences. Moreover, students were permitted to choose from among some electives, although the choice was limited by the small number of courses offered. To provide guidance to students and to replicate the academic environment they would face upon transfer to the United States, the MUCIA faculty and staff in Shah Alam established a student academic advising unit consisting of ITM project staff and expatriate volunteers. These efforts were consistent with the stated mission of the program to train Malaysian students in the style of learning necessary for successful completion of upper-division academic programs in the United States.

While ITM agreed to the curricular plan that MUCIA initially proposed, the range of courses and choice afforded students ran counter to the institution's own approach. At ITM, the curriculum focused narrowly on technical skills and afforded little choice among courses. ITM staff reasoned that by accepting a scholarship for a specific field of study, students had committed themselves to that field and need not "experiment" with courses in other areas. By the end of the second year of the program, the institutional culture at ITM began to manifest itself in the form of pressure to drop the individual humanities courses in the MUCIA program as well as the general studies requirements of the A.G.S. degree. Some ITM administrators also questioned the need for a student

≋ It was often difficult to separate key administrative and management decisions from their effects on the academic program and vice versa.

advising unit, suggesting that a simple publication would suffice since course sequences should be fixed in advance. Apart from a differing philosophy of education, reducing the program's cost was an added incentive for these proposed changes. While the argument in favor of a student advising unit prevailed, some course electives were eventually dropped from the curriculum.

Complex Lines of Decision-Making Authority

On the home campus, deans make virtually all important decisions regarding quality assurance, although some major decisions also require approval from more senior university administrators. For the IU portion of the program, decision-making authority regarding academic matters rested with the IU unit that provided the curriculum. Initially, this was the IU School of Continuing Studies (based at IU-Bloomington) and later the Undergraduate Education Center on the campus of Indiana University-Purdue University Indianapolis.

Internally at IU, program finances and day-to-day operations were managed by the Office of International Programs (OIP) because of its prior experience in such projects and a direct reporting line to the Office of the President. Finally, the provost of the ITM/MUCIA program administered the program on site and reported to IU on academic matters and to MUCIA on contractual matters. As noted previously, MUCIA was the prime contractor and IU, as lead institution, subcontracted with MUCIA to offer the program.

While the division of decision-making authority between academic and financial administrators outlined above was warranted by circumstances, it was often difficult to separate key administrative and management decisions from their effects on the academic program and vice versa. There were thus four parties that could claim final authority over at least some matters on the U.S. side of the program: the IU home campus issuing the transcript, the Office of International Programs, the provost in Shah Alam, and MUCIA, represented by its Executive Office.

Management of the program on the Malaysian side was similarly complex. The Institut Teknologi MARA was charged with providing local administrative support and logistics for the program. Funding, however, was provided by the Malaysian Department of Public Service from funds appropriated for national scholarship programs. The Ministry of Education, which oversaw the Institut Teknologi MARA, the Malaysian Treasury Department, which disbursed project funds, and the Malaysian Attorney General's Office, which approved government contracts and agreements also held key policy and financial stakes in the project. As with the U.S. side, agendas and interests among the Malaysian participants sometimes differed. On both sides, it was difficult at times to determine who on the "other side" held final decision-making authority over certain matters.

When yearly negotiations on the renewal of the project were conducted, therefore, each of these parties was present and had to be consulted on major decisions. Formal negotiations resembled a United Nations gathering. A total of anywhere from 9 to 13 people from the two sides could be involved in the formal meetings. As a result, annual negotiations on project renewal frequently took six to eight months. The focus of these exercises became the details of the next year's budget rather than longer-term planning. Distributed lines of authority on both sides of the program thus rendered decision making time-consuming and complex.

Recruitment, Development, and Retention
of Malaysian Instructors
The immediate need in Malaysia in 1985 for skilled manpower dictated sending students abroad. At the time of the program's initiation, Malaysian participants spoke only generally of the possibility that ITM might some day operate the program on its own. Scant attention was given to this, however, until a recession in 1987 accelerated the need to achieve cost savings through the increased use of Malaysian instructors. For the following several years, political uncertainties and other issues postponed formal efforts to institutionalize the program at ITM as either an ITM/MUCIA partnership or operated solely by ITM.

Delays in the implementation of long-term plans for the center were manifested in several ways:

1. The site that the ITM/MUCIA Center occupied had been a secondary school. When the program began, the state and federal governments were in dispute over which entity held legal title to the land. As a result, the construction of new facilities had to be delayed several years until the matter could be resolved.

≋ The problem was to determine what minimum level of funding was required to maintain quality assurance in the program.

2. Lacking approval as a permanent ITM program, faculty positions for Malaysian instructors at the ITM/MUCIA Center could not be created as permanent civil service appointments. Instead, Malaysian faculty were hired on short-term, annually renewable contracts with modest salaries and few benefits. Lacking a long-term employment commitment, some of the best-qualified instructors left the program for more secure positions.

3. Given their status as "external hires," Malaysian faculty were not eligible during the first few years of the program for the faculty development grants available to regular ITM faculty, which provided travel to professional meetings abroad and scholarships for advanced study.

4. While academic research was valued by ITM administrators, there were few incentives in the ITM/MUCIA program for either Malaysian or U.S. faculty to conduct or publish research. Further, access to funds and facilities for research was limited.

ITM administrators were well aware of these problems but were unable to effect changes in the early years of the program until policy decisions were made at higher levels.

To mitigate some of these problems, IU and MUCIA both provided funds for scholarships for advanced studies in the United States and for short-term visits to the United States for ITM faculty and staff. In addition, IU/MUCIA faculty offered the noncredit faculty seminars, graduate courses on site, and mentoring and practice teaching programs described above. After five years of program operation, the Malaysian federal government secured legal title to the land on which the facility was located. A policy decision was then made to continue the program on a long-term basis with local faculty and staff accorded regular civil service teaching appointments with full rights and benefits.

Over time, the efforts made by ITM and IU/MUCIA helped to increase opportunities for the professional development of Malaysian instructors in the program. More recently, the Ministry of Education granted approval for ITM to offer degrees as well as diplomas. In the future, this will enhance ITM's ability to attract and retain greater numbers of qualified faculty. During the life of the ITM/MUCIA program, however, the salary structure at ITM—as a diploma-granting institution—made it less competitive in the search for new faculty than Malaysian universities, which could offer higher salaries. As a practical matter, increasing the number of Malaysian instructors in the program in order to reduce the number and cost of U.S. instructors—a prime objective of the Malaysian administrators—proved challenging.

Financial Issues

At the outset, Malaysian administrators made clear that one objective of the program was to reduce the cost of overseas instruction for government-sponsored students. All parties assumed that offering the instruction on site in Malaysia would reduce the cost of the first two years of instruction as well as the loss of money due to poor foreign exchange rates. Not until the program was more than two years old, however, could Malaysian or MUCIA administrators predict, with certainty, the key parameters of program cost. The unpredictable parameters included such things as the number of students admissible to the program, the average length of time needed to complete English-language study, student retention rates, and the distribution of students across different majors and courses. For its part, MUCIA elected to negotiate a cost reimbursable contract (meaning that any savings would be returned to Malaysia). Concerned lest the negotiated agreement provide insufficient operating funds, MUCIA and IU estimated costs liberally, knowing that any excess would be returned. As a countervailing concern, the need for cost savings became more urgent and imperative for the Malaysian side in the midst of the 1987 recession.

In addition, by 1987 ITM had initiated twinning programs with three other U.S. consortia or institutions. The idea was to facilitate the placement of students in different regions of the United States. The main consequence of this arrangement, however, was to spur competition on the basis of cost, quality, and service between the four U.S. programs. This coincided with a government decision in 1987 to cut the number of scholarships for overseas study in half, thus dramatically reducing the number of students who could participate in the twinning programs. ITM then let it be known that it was no longer efficient for it to operate four twinning programs and that three of them would soon have to be closed down. In addition, Australian, British, and other U.S. universities began to initiate twinning programs in Malaysia in partnership with private institutions. The Malaysian partners of these programs lobbied the government for a share of the government-sponsored students and cited lower costs as the primary advantage of their programs. In their quest to reduce costs, ITM administrators thus soon had a wealth of competing models and programs with which to compare the MUCIA program.

MUCIA and IU met the challenge to reduce costs through improved economies of scale, efficiencies in management, and the addition of increasing numbers of IU-approved Malaysian instructors. For IU and MUCIA, the problem was to determine what minimum level of funding was required to maintain quality assurance in the program. Over a period of approximately three years and after extensive discussions that included academic administrators at IU-Bloomington and IUPUI, MUCIA board members, and the MUCIA executive staff, a consensus emerged (discussed in the following section). Using this as a basis for negotiating program costs with Malaysian counterparts, MUCIA determined the bottom line, beyond which it was not willing to go to achieve cost reductions. In the end, Malaysian decision makers decided to select the IU/MUCIA program, on the basis of program quality and service, as ITM's long-term partner.

Program "Character" and Faculty Accountability

A key element in quality assurance is the ability to periodically review faculty performance coupled with the ability to influence it when necessary. This includes reward or punishment through salary and other employment-related benefits. With regard to the terms of employment for Malaysian faculty, Malaysian instructors teaching in the IU program were subject to employment rules that emanated from the Malaysian civil service. Salary raises, contractual terms, employment obligations, and related matters were thus determined by ITM administrators according to civil service regulations. Thus, while these faculty taught IU courses, they were not directly accountable to MUCIA administrators for their teaching performance or professional development once they were appointed to the program.

Initially, nearly 100 percent of the faculty teaching in the program were appointed by Indiana University from among the core and regional campuses of MUCIA member institutions. Following the 1987 recession, for the reasons outlined above, the Institut Teknologi MARA requested the hiring of more Malaysian faculty. By 1992 approximately 45 percent of the instruction was provided by Malaysian teachers.

With increasing numbers of Malaysian staff, the character of the program changed gradually to reflect Malaysian traditions and values in higher education. As their numbers grew, Malaysian instructors increasingly looked to the standards, policies, and procedures of the Institut Teknologi MARA rather than Indiana University as their peer and professional reference points. This was neither unusual nor unexpected under the circumstances. Some U.S. observers worried, however, that ITM/MUCIA students, having had fewer U.S. instructors, would experience greater "academic culture shock" when transferring to U.S. upper-division programs.

Some of these concerns proved unfounded. Students transferring to the United States continued to perform well in upper-division programs long after significant numbers of Malaysian instructors joined the program. Studies by program staff of the academic performance of transfer students in 1992 and 1993 indicated that academic culture shock did not manifest itself in the upper-division grade-point averages of these students. In any case, the increasing numbers of Malaysian faculty served the objective of preparing ITM to assume full academic control of the program.

The change in the proportion of U.S. to Malaysian faculty, however, presented IU with a dilemma: At what point would the ITM/MUCIA Center become an ITM program and no longer an IU program? Discussions about the character of the program never involved the qualifications of the Malaysian faculty, however, since they had already been evaluated and approved by IU. Rather, the issues concerned accountability to the program and transcript and determination of the point at which the program no longer offered an American-style education comparable to that offered by IU or other MUCIA universities.

For some, resolution of these issues revolved around the question of whether IU retained "meaningful control" of the academic program. Meaningful control in this context meant accountability, i.e., the ability to influence faculty behavior through incentives, rewards, and peer pressure with the objective of improving teaching, service, and research. Some senior administrators at IU and MUCIA felt that a U.S.-to-Malaysian faculty ratio of 80-20 percent already represented a significant loss of accountability; others felt that a 60-40 percent ratio represented the point at which IU could no longer ensure accountability. For other decision makers, the issue was less about accountability and more about the character of the program changing from American to Malaysian.

In the end, both IU administrators and the MUCIA board decided that a 50-50 percent ratio was one at which a meaningful partnership and collaboration in a U.S.-style undergraduate program could continue. Senior ITM administrators concurred in this decision. Thereafter, the faculty ratio served for the U.S. side as a logical point of departure after which the program's U.S.-style instruction began to change substantially. Moreover, it came to be viewed as the point at which increased participation of local instructors effectively transferred responsibility for quality assurance (grading standards, adherence to syllabi, etc.) from IU to ITM hands. At that point, it seemed appropriate that the ITM transcript be substituted for the IU transcript.

When the ITM/MUCIA program was in the planning stages in 1984, neither side could have discussed these transition issues in any concrete way. The immediacy of organizing and launching the program precluded consideration of how (or even whether) a transition to ITM administration could eventually be achieved. What made informed decision making possible later on was effective monitoring of program outcomes. The key output measures were the quality of placements in the United States for transferring students and their academic performance once enrolled in upper-division programs. Since the program remained strong on both measures, decision makers at IU and MUCIA agreed to increased Malaysian faculty participation. However, once the ratios of Malaysian and U.S. faculty reached near parity, considerations of accountability and the program's changing character necessitated a decision on the level of MUCIA faculty participation appropriate for continued use of the IU transcript.

Transition to an ITM Transcript

ITM and IU discussed two approaches to effecting a transition to the ITM transcript: (1) cease issuing an IU transcript when ITM's cohort in the *total* faculty exceeded 50 percent, or (2) gradually move courses on a discipline-by-discipline basis from IU's transcript to ITM's transcript as the percentage of ITM-employed faculty teaching in *each* discipline exceeded 50 percent. The first approach would have provided an earlier transition to the ITM transcript, but would have presented two problems. First, an abrupt transition from the IU to the ITM transcript could have had a negative impact on the placement of transfer students in U.S. institutions. Second, ITM was concerned about its ability to recruit replacements for 50 percent of the faculty if the MUCIA partnership ceased abruptly. In the end, IU, MUCIA, and ITM agreed to the second, more gradual plan with the proviso that when MUCIA was providing only 25 percent of the total faculty, the remaining disciplines would be moved to the ITM transcript.

Once the procedure was fully understood by everyone, it was implemented with little difficulty. Indeed, the process had begun earlier in business, psychology, and chemistry. When more than 50 percent of the instruction in these disciplines was being offered by ITM-employed faculty, these courses were moved to ITM's transcript. In each of these disciplines, enrollments were small and only one or two faculty members taught in any given semester. The hiring of a single Malaysian faculty member in these disciplines, therefore, immediately tilted the balance of instruction in favor of ITM. The faculty teaching these courses were still the same ones that IU had approved to teach, only now they did so with ITM validating the course work.

Computer science was the next discipline to be moved to the ITM transcript. During this period of transition, students transferred to the U.S. institutions with two transcripts: one recording their work in the ITM-supervised disciplines and one their work in the IU-supervised courses. Several MUCIA faculty continued teaching courses in disciplines that now appeared on the ITM transcript until Malaysian replacements could be recruited. At the same time, IU-appointed Malaysian staff continued teaching alongside MUCIA faculty in courses appearing on the IU transcript.

The program reached the point in 1995 when only 25 percent of the total faculty was employed by MUCIA, and the ITM/MUCIA Cooperative Program gave way to the ITM American Diploma Program (ITM-ADP). To avoid confusion, IU and ITM worked together from 1993 on to inform U.S. admission officers of the transition taking place. Catalogs of syllabi for both the IU and ITM-ADP programs were distributed annually explaining the transition and indicating transcript changes. IU and ITM staff also made presentations at the annual meetings of university admission officers and international educators. In addition, an ITM-ADP

≋ When guidance of any other kind was lacking, the ITM/MUCIA program based policy decisions on the likely impact of the decisions on the program's output measures.

staff member interned for one year in the MUCIA Placement Office at IU to learn firsthand the process by which students from the Shah Alam site gained transfer admission to upper-division bachelor's degree programs in the United States. This staff member then moved to the offices of the Malaysian Students Department in Washington, D.C., to assume full responsibility for placing ITM-ADP graduates in U.S. institutions.

Lessons Learned
The basic organizational principles that apply to accreditation of off-campus academic programs in the United States served to guide the establishment of the ITM/MUCIA Cooperative Program in Malaysia. These principles could not, however, provide guidance on how to address key quality assurance issues in the nontraditional environment of twinning programs. In the life of the ITM/MUCIA Program, these issues included such things as contractual relationships between contractor and subcontractor, lines of authority for academic decision making, the implementation of institution-building plans in the absence of resources and policy decisions, faculty development in the context of short-term contracts, the accountability of local faculty employed by a U.S. host institution, and procedures for program termination that protect the interests of all participants.

The publication of *Principles of Good Practice in Overseas International Education Programs for Non-U.S. Nationals* by the Council on Post-secondary Accreditation in 1990 and more recent efforts, such as the standards outlined in Chapter 8, provide comprehensive guidance based on the real-world experiences of U.S. overseas programs. Such principles cannot, however, anticipate every circumstance in which twinning programs might operate. When guidance of any other kind was lacking, the ITM/MUCIA program based policy decisions on the likely impact of the decisions on the program's output measures, i.e., student academic performance in Shah Alam and at U.S. institutions. Whenever possible, changes were implemented slowly and with the full involvement of faculty at Indiana University. In addition, the impact of these changes on the program's output measures was carefully monitored. This monitoring included the analysis of grading trends in Shah Alam each semester and the periodic gathering and analyzing of data on as many as 1,500 U.S. transcripts. Without the staff resources to evaluate the performance of transfer students in the United States, a key element in assessing program quality would have been lost.

For many years U.S. educators have raised concerns about the practices of some U.S. universities with respect to their offshore academic programs. In the competitive, rapidly growing higher education environment of Malaysia, it is especially important for U.S. institutions to establish the best quality assurance standards possible; most U.S. programs, past and present, have done so. In the choice of its host partner institution, the ITM/MUCIA Cooperative Program was especially fortunate. Increased competition from British and Australian programs and the financial motives of the many for-profit twinning programs in Malaysia, however, may provide temptations to bend quality assurance standards to the breaking point. It would take only one significant, public failure of a U.S. twinning program to render significant damage to the reputation of U.S. higher education in Malaysia. Concerned over the unregulated conduct of private colleges in Malaysia, the Malaysian Parliament enacted new legislation in 1996 that requires the registration of private colleges and establishes new procedures for the accreditation of both public and private institutions of higher education. While these measures will undoubtedly help to protect Malaysian consumers of higher education, it is incumbent upon U.S. higher education institutions offering offshore academic programs to regulate themselves.

Charles Reafsnyder is associate dean for International Research and Development at Indiana University. Between 1985–92 he held several positions with the ITM/MUCIA Cooperative Program in Malaysia—a two-year undergraduate program that offered Indiana University credits in Malaysia. Since then, he has been involved in the evaluation and planning of other U.S. academic programs abroad, and in national seminars on the issue of the accreditation of overseas U.S. programs.

CHAPTER 7

The Value of Standards Within the Home Institutional Setting

John H. Yopp
Associate Vice Chancellor for Academic Affairs
and Dean of the Graduate School
Southern Illinois University at Carbondale

Rhonda Vinson
Executive Assistant to the Chancellor
for International Affairs and Economic Development
Southern Illinois University at Carbondale

International initiatives leading to the offering of credit-bearing programs abroad have frequently been among the more entrepreneurial and controversial of the ventures undertaken by U.S. institutions of higher education over the past two decades. While many such programs have become an integral and valued component of the missions of certain institutions, some have led to unanticipated academic, budgetary, and public relations problems.

The basic premise of this discussion is that these unanticipated consequences can be minimized, or even prevented, by institutional utilization of a set of guidelines or standards during the initial stages of the negotiating process.

Experiences that serve to illustrate this premise derive in part from the diverse collaborative international activities engaged in over the years by Southern Illinois University at Carbondale (SIUC). Other illustrative experiences have been reported over the past 10 years by faculty and administrators from internationally active universities at meetings of professional associations concerned with international education.

The first U.S. student visa ever issued was for a South Korean student to attend SIUC in 1947. In the last two decades, SIUC has enrolled students from over 100 countries and stayed in the top-20 ranking for numbers of international students enrolled. SIUC's international relationships have increased to include 80 linkage agreements with colleges and universities in 43 countries, and have resulted in over $80 million in external funding. SIUC's collaborative efforts are diverse and include

≋ The basic premise of this discussion is that these unanticipated consequences can be minimized, or even prevented, by institutional utilization of a set of guidelines or standards during the initial stages of the negotiating process.

coal research with faculty from Russia, technical training for workers in industries in Korea, curriculum development with medical schools in Peru, teacher training with the Education Ministry in Nepal, and a joint Master's of Business Administration (M.B.A.) diploma with a university in France. In the past 8 to 10 years, these international relationships have stimulated an interest in the development of programs that offer academic credit at international sites. The off-campus SIUC program in Nakajo, Niigata, Japan, is a fine example of a collaborative effort between the academic community and a city and prefectural government.

The difficulty or ease of establishing and maintaining quality in international educational efforts can be correlated with the use of standards, which serve to enhance and clarify communications among parties.

An excellent example of guidelines for institutions to utilize in negotiations on establishing credit-bearing courses or programs abroad are the *Standards for U.S. Institutions Offering Credit-Bearing Programs Abroad* (see Chapter 8, referred to hereafter as the "standards"). SIUC has used these standards, and found them to be effective, in negotiations with private and public partners seeking to establish academic programs in other countries.

It is useful to distinguish, for discussion purposes, between the general value of having a coherent, organized set of standards and the particular value of this specific set of standards.

Standards can provide an information source explaining overall university policy for negotiators who are not in academic affairs administration. At many institutions, representatives with decision-making authority negotiating an international program are not familiar with all of their institution's policies governing credit-bearing instruction abroad. In some cases, representatives of international programs do not report to the provost or academic vice president. This lack of a direct link to the academic (course-delivering) units of the university may lead to serious information gaps.

Providing the hosts desiring in-country delivery of instruction with a set of printed materials and standards will facilitate preliminary discussions. These printed standards become even more useful when the hosts, whether they represent the public or private sector, present the proposed program plans to others who will become involved, e.g., investors, university officials, government officials, and/or funding agencies (World Bank, etc.).

Printed standards can also become the catalyst at the home campus for establishing closer links between nonacademic international development administrators and the academic community through advisory councils, jointly appointed committees, and contact personnel designated by college deans.

Standards represent a valuable negotiation guide for discussions with third-party providers. There has been a rapid growth in the number of third-party organizations offering (and soliciting) to broker international programs in selected countries. These providers frequently contact colleges, departments, or even faculty directly for program delivery on a cost-recovery (i.e., non-tuition generating) basis.

Third-party arrangements often look attractive because they are thought to be less subject to university policies and accreditation requirements. In fact, they generally are not. In addition, negotiations with third-party providers often move quickly and go outside the mainstream of ordinary procedures for approval. Each academic unit of the university should be provided with a set of standards to give to the third party before agreements are negotiated. This prevents unrealistic expectations on the part of all parties and avoids the need to extricate faculty from involvement in programs that do not meet university standards.

Standards can also be an information source for ministries of education or university affairs. Approval for delivery of courses or programs in a particular country often involves negotiations with the ministry of education. This may be the case even if a third-party provider is involved. It is particularly likely if a degree is to be granted.

Developing countries often seek guidance in establishing standards for courses or programs to be delivered by a U.S. institution. Other, more developed countries, may have their own educational standards and policies firmly in place, but these may clash with those of the U.S. institution. Serious misunderstandings leading at best to "loss of face" for the parties involved can, and do, occur as a consequence. Standards offer an excellent way to establish common understandings on which to base negotiations with official bodies in the host country.

Standards provide a mechanism to facilitate negotiations that involve faculty. It is always desirable to inform the faculty to be involved in the program abroad before any negotiations take place. It is likewise desirable to consider faculty-based procedures for approval when drafting agreements, since faculty are responsible for the content and quality of their courses.

If faculty have before them the standards as a set of procedures to approve through their governance structures (i.e., faculty senate and/or graduate council), mistrust and misunderstandings during the approval process can be avoided. The approval process will also go faster because the standards encompass the policies of the major institutional units involved (e.g., admission, legal counsel, etc.).

Standards can help elicit the approval and support of national and state legislators and governing and coordinating boards for international initiatives. Past commitments to international educational activities are being questioned by some legislators in Congress and in state government. State coordinating boards of higher education are also challenging the quality and integrity of programs abroad.

One frequently voiced concern is that students in a particular course or program delivered abroad are admitted on the basis of less stringent admission requirements than those in place at the home institution. A further concern is that, once admitted, these students are judged by lower standards. These, and other related concerns, can be addressed by providing national and state legislators, state coordinating boards, and institutional governing boards with a set of standards. This allows them, in turn, to give clear answers to their concerned constituents. Standard 3 and its substandards, "Marketing of and Admission to the Course/Program Offerings," corresponds to these concerns.

Legislators and higher education coordinating boards often ask how an institution's international activities relate to its stated mission and to the oft-lauded "internationalization" of the institution.

Standards represent a source of information for program review. In most instances, the programs delivered abroad are the same in course content as those delivered on the home campus in the United States. External and internal reviewers who regularly evaluate campus programs require information on how content, delivery, and quality are assured for programs offered abroad. In the case of regional accrediting associations, standards are often requested before the course or program can be offered. With respect to the North Central Association of Colleges and

Schools, a set of standards or principles for credit-bearing instruction abroad has already been promulgated. Any set of standards, including that discussed here, must be consistent with that of the relevant accrediting body. Standard 2.b and the subsections of Standard 6 address these issues.

A survey of chief academic officers of universities belonging to the Oak Ridge Associated Universities (ORAU) consortium was conducted to solicit opinions about the standards presented in this book. The survey was undertaken by ORAU's International Committee. All respondents to the survey indicated either that their institutions were already using very similar standards or that they believed the standards were an excellent guide and should be used.

Home-institution control of marketing is particularly important in for-profit ventures involving third-party providers. The profit to the parties depends on the number of students enrolled. Pressure may, therefore, be exerted to use advertising in an inappropriate way. Such advertising may not make it clear which party controls the admission process and requirements.

Even in the case of publicly sponsored ventures, political pressure can be strong for host-government officials to justify expenditure of public funds, leading to the potential for confused signals to students and parents. Home-institution control of marketing can ensure that the student is receiving clear, accurate information. If a public entity, especially a ministry of education, is sponsoring or sanctioning the program abroad, students may assume that their degree will be granted by that ministry. In those cases where a ministry requires that it issue a document to students certifying that they have completed the requirements set by in-country law to graduate, control of marketing materials by the U.S. institution is crucial. The student must understand that the diploma is granted in completion of the U.S. institution's requirements and that the accompanying document is issued by the host government because it recognizes the U.S. institution's standards.

The marketing approach must also make it clear that the U.S. institution determines admission, sets academic requirements, and keeps the official student records, which may not be released to anyone without the permission of the student. Standards can help prevent potential legal conflicts that may emerge between policies governing the rights of students in the United States and the host country by making it clear that students in the host country are students of the U.S. institution.

Home institutions must ensure that there is a market for their proposed program in the host country. U.S. institutions need to know very early in the negotiation process the educational background of prospective students. Unfortunately, this can quite easily be misrepresented by the party abroad marketing the program. Desire for a degree is not necessarily correlated with level of previous educational achievement. Therefore, attention to Standard 3.d is particularly important in the earliest stages of negotiation. Standard 2.c is, likewise, important to the development of a marketing strategy.

The proposed standards support the need for market research to determine if there is a need for the proposed program in the host country. Potential partners abroad, whether private or public, may hesitate to conduct the appropriate needs surveys to accurately assess the availability of qualified students in numbers sufficient to make a program cost effective. A valid market study will determine the number of students with adequate academic qualifications to be admitted, the number of students interested in the proposed program, and future demographics to evaluate the long-term need for such a program. Accrediting bodies are requiring more in-depth assessment of need through market research than in the past. The numerous closings of overseas programs, especially in Japan, underscore the importance of conducting market studies in advance.

One of the pitfalls of accelerated negotiation is inadequate assessment of the human resources needed to support the proposed program. This assessment is a very complex task that must involve home faculty and department administrators. Questions of departmental capacity to offer the home curriculum, the disadvantages for faculty of teaching abroad, and the impact on the quality of home courses, especially at the undergraduate level, are but a few that must be answered. The subsections of Standard 4 address these issues.

This issue is of particular importance to accrediting agencies such as the North Central Association and other bodies that accredit specific academic programs, such as the American Assembly of Collegiate Schools of Business.

Physical facilities in the host country should be comparable to those at the U.S. institution. Standards 5.a and 5.b address this concern, which is particularly relevant to programs offered through a third-party provider on a for-profit basis in developing countries. Although the physical facilities to support instruction and student needs may not be identical to those in the United States, such facilities must meet standards for safety established by the U.S. Environmental Protection Agency (EPA) and OSHA. In cases in which physical facilities are to be constructed, the U.S. institution should work with the architect(s) involved to assure that these standards are met.

The authors hope that the issues raised and experiences described provide convincing evidence of the need to adopt the standards outlined in this publication, or a similar set of guiding standards, when proposing the establishment of credit-bearing instruction abroad. It is exceedingly difficult to anticipate all of the valid concerns of the diverse constituencies described in this chapter that are to be served by these standards. However, a university's reputation in the international arena is determined, for better or for worse, by the degree of integrity of the standards employed in the negotiating process. In addition, as John Deupree has outlined in Chapter 1, the stakes are higher than just those of individual institutional integrity.

John H. Yopp is associate vice chancellor for Research and dean of the Graduate School at Southern Illinois University at Carbondale. He has long been involved in the international dimensions of graduate education. He has served or currently serves on the Council of Graduate Schools Board, the GRE Board, the TOEFL Policy Council (chair), the Council on Research Policy and Graduate Education of the National Association of State Universities and Land Grant Colleges (past chair), the National Liaison Committee (chair), the Executive Deans Committee for ATLAS/AFGRAD of the African American Institute, and the Council for the Center for Quality Assurance in International Education.

Rhonda Vinson is the executive assistant to the chancellor for International Affairs and Economic Development at Southern Illinois University at Carbondale.

CHAPTER 8

A Voluntary Presentation of Standards for U.S. Institutions Offering Credit-Bearing Programs Abroad

The following standards for U.S. institutions offering credit-bearing programs abroad are offered as a self-managed, regulatory tool for voluntary adoption by institutions. As detailed in Chapter 2, the standards were drafted by a group of concerned individuals who had been involved in the national symposium "Does U.S. Higher Education Need a Foreign Policy?" held June 20–21, 1994, in Princeton, New Jersey and subsequent related meetings. (A list of participants in the symposium is attached in Appendix 1.)

Since their original drafting the standards have been circulated informally among a number of institutional representatives. They have been presented to sessions at the Association of International Education Administrators. They were also presented to the executive directors of the regional accrediting bodies who discussed them at the January 1995 meeting in San Diego, California.

Based upon the informal circulation of these standards, many observations and expressions of support have been forwarded to the Center for Quality Assurance in International Education.

A presentation of the standards follows.

1. Goals and Objectives of the Course/Program Offerings

1.a The institution providing the course/program offerings in an international setting describes clearly and publicly the goals and objectives of those offerings.

1.b These goals and objectives relate to and support the institution's more broadly stated mission and purposes.

1.c The goals and objectives of the course/program offerings identify how they address educational needs of students and of the host country.

2. Content, Structure, and Rigor of the Course/Program Offerings

2.a The institution documents the acceptance by the appropriate home-campus governance bodies of the content, structure, and rigor of the course/program offerings.

2.b The home institution applies to the course/program offerings the same standards it applies to programs on the home campus, including those required by institutional and specialized accrediting bodies.

2.c The course/program offerings, when appropriate, include content relevant to student needs as defined by the culture of the host country.

2.d The home institution both establishes and assures the achievement of the language proficiencies required for admission to and/or completion of the course/program offerings.

3. Marketing of and Admission to the Course/Program Offerings

3.a The home institution assures that the marketing program abroad provides to prospective international students truthful information about the course/program offerings and their place in the broader U.S. higher education community.

3.b The marketing program abroad clearly identifies and accurately explains any contractual arrangements made by the home institution to provide the course/program offerings.

3.c The home institution establishes and publishes the admission requirements for its international course/program offerings. It justifies differences between them and stated requirements for admission of international students to the home campus.

3.d The admission requirements reflect an appropriate understanding of the educational system of the host country.

Ambassadors of U.S. Higher Education

4. Human Resources to Support the Course/Program Offerings

4.a The administrative structures and personnel of the home campus are capable of fulfilling the institution's responsibilities for oversight of the course/program offerings.

4.b A resident director, employed by the home institution, provides primary oversight of the course/program offerings and reports directly to a designated academic administrator at the home campus.

4.c The teaching faculty at the international site possess academic credentials appropriate to the level of instruction and the content of the courses.

4.d The staff and teaching faculty, if not educated in the United States, have sufficient experience with U.S. higher education to assure that its practices and values inform the international operation.

4.e The home-campus systems of evaluation and reward recognize the contributions of staff and teaching faculty recruited from the home campus to serve at an international site.

4.f The home institution assures that the teaching faculty and support staff at the international site have the language proficiency(ies) necessary to fulfill their responsibilities.

4.g The home institution assures that the appointment and review processes for faculty and staff meet guidelines of the home campus and, where necessary, conform to relevant laws in the host country.

5. Financial and Physical Resources to Support the Course/Program Offerings

5.a The home institution provides its course/program offerings in physical facilities that meet, if not exceed, the facilities typical for quality higher education in the host country.

≋ *The home institution incorporates its international courses/programs into the review processes required by external agencies, including institutional and specialized accrediting associations.*

5.b The physical facilities in international settings assure students access to and use of the learning resources—including information services, computers, and laboratories—requisite to the content and rigor of the course/program offerings.

5.c The home institution documents that its financial arrangements, including those defined in contracts, provide adequate and dependable support for the international course/program offerings.

5.d The home institution requires that a contracting entity provides for its review and the review of accreditors' documentation of the expenditure of tuition and fees charged students enrolled in the international course/program offerings.

5.e The home institution has contingency plans showing its capacity, if necessary, to fulfill its obligations to all students admitted to its international courses/programs.

6. Evaluation of the Course/Program Offerings

6.a The home institution documents that student transcripts for international course/program offerings accurately reflect student learning and truthfully inform all who use the transcripts about the content and rigor of the courses/programs as well as the site of instruction.

6.b The home institution documents that its governing board regularly reviews the international course/program offerings.

6.c The home institution integrates the evaluation of its international course/program offerings into its on-going activities of program review.

6.d The home institution assures that its program review structures allow faculty and staff at international sites a role in evaluating and strengthening the courses/programs in which they participate.

6.e The home institution incorporates its international courses/ programs into the review processes required by external agencies, including institutional and specialized accrediting associations.

CHAPTER 9

Postlude: University Education Enters a Fourth Dimension

Philip J. Palin
The Laurasian Institution

The university is undergoing a fundamental transformation. A half-century ago the massification of U.S. higher education altered the university significantly. The changes of the next 50 years will be even more profound.

Three factors are driving the current transformation: the globalization of the economy, increasing demand for tertiary (postsecondary) education throughout the world, and widespread access to education through technology.

The previous chapters have illustrated how the first two factors are already exerting their influence. In Chapter 2 Marjorie Peace Lenn outlines how the General Agreement on Trade in Services (GATS) and other international trade agreements encouraged "the development of common educational standards, mutual recognition, and liberalization of the licensing and certification processes by which professionals are allowed to practice." Education is a principal component of economic development and, in the most advanced economies, a major economic sector in itself. As such, education is a principal focus of economic policymaking. While this is not new, the economic perspective is coming to prevail over the social, civil, and intellectual perspectives.

Architecture is a good example of a global profession. Whereas 20 years ago only a very few of the best-known architects could claim an international practice, there are now hundreds of firms engaged in cross-border transactions. The same can be said of accounting, engineering, law, and other service professions. In Chapter 4 John Maudlin-Jeronimo notes that there is work underway to have in place by 1999 an "Accord on International Minimum Standards of Professionalism in Architectural Practice." The proposed agreement will "include standards for both education and accreditation."

Global economic growth is stimulating an increased demand for professional services. These services are available principally in mature economies, which over several generations have developed the educational and regulatory infrastructure to sustain and advance the professions. In most professional service areas, sources of excess supply are geographically distant from the locus of demand (e.g., Los Angeles and Seoul). In such circumstances, demand is often filled by local providers and quality is below accepted professional standards. It is in the self-interest of both the customer and the profession that minimum quality be maintained.

To accommodate localized supply with globalized demand and offer a reasonable assurance of quality, we are now witnessing a number of international discussions and agreements that essentially address three issues:

• Minimum global standards for professional education and practice;

• Creation of an open international market for professional services; and

• Enhancing access to professional services through global engagement in the development of localized capacity, especially through local professional education and development programs.

This process of globalization is most fully advanced in the professional service sector and in professional education, but it will have a significant impact on all of tertiary education. In Chapter 6 Charles Reafsnyder in his case study describes a Malaysian economy that is incredibly robust and in which the demand for skilled workers far exceeds the supply. He observes that "the government of Malaysia recently announced plans for five large government-owned corporations to establish their own diploma and degree-granting programs. In response, each of these companies established relationships with overseas 'twinning' partners." The Malaysian policy is reflective of higher education initiatives in many of the most dynamic economies. Ministries of education and culture are often resistant, but more powerful ministries related to finance, trade, or the economy have often concluded that drawing on the educational capacity of the United States, Australia, and others is a necessary option for developing the human resources that their economic growth requires.

The experience of U.S. branch schools in Japan is, however, a cautionary tale for both education providers and consumers. In Chapter 5 Jared H. Dorn has provided a helpful discussion of the dangers involved when market forces dilute educational quality. It is debatable whether in the late 1980s there was a widespread *need* for U.S. branch schools in Japan, but there was undoubtedly unsatisfied market demand for higher education among the Japanese. For the various reasons outlined by Dorn and others, over 30 U.S. tertiary institutions entered Japan over a period of a few years, in what the Japanese media often compared to a "gold rush." While each institution encountered a unique set of circumstances, the best admit it was a struggle to maintain quality. Unfortunately, many institutions barely tried. The failure by several, perhaps most, of the U.S. branch campuses in Japan to maintain appropriate educational standards contributed substantially to the closure of all but a few. Moreover, as the reputation for poor quality grew it had a negative impact even on those institutions, such as SIUC in Niigata, that were committed to educational quality.

Quality assurance processes should, I would argue, focus on ensuring that the student receives an education consistent with what the institution communicates as its mission, purpose, and policy. But quality assurance serves other ends as well. The experiences of U.S. branch schools in Japan have been observed by educational policymakers elsewhere in the Asia-Pacific region, and have clearly encouraged caution in Korea, Thailand, and elsewhere. In the case of the U.S. university operating abroad, rigorous quality assurance mechanisms are essential to ensure that the reputation of U.S. higher education is maintained. Education is what is known as an "intangible product," and an essential element of such a product's success is its reputation.

The quality of the U.S. higher education system is currently perceived as very high. It is in the self-interest of all stakeholders to ensure that this reputation is both accurate and preserved.

Implications of Economic Globalization for Tertiary Education

The image of the multilingual, cross-culturally competent, international professional has excited the imagination of many educators. But while there is a real need for many more such individuals, demand can

≋ The most profound result of economic globalization is the integration of millions of new producers and consumers as full participants in the international economy.

probably be measured in the thousands, certainly not in the hundreds of thousands. It is an error to assume that economic globalization implies that daily economic life will become increasingly cosmopolitan. It will for a few more, but not for most.

Paul Krugman and others have pointed out that, compared with a century ago, an increasing proportion of the work force is engaged in providing services that are consumed locally. "Most people . . . don't sell their wares to distant customers. Instead, most of the employment is in those 'non-base' activities, goods and (especially) services that are provided by local workers, to local consumers, for local consumption."[1] The export base of a local economy is the foundation of its prosperity, but it may only employ about a quarter of the work force. And even among those directly engaged in producing for the export base, not every employee of an export-oriented firm, such as Caterpillar, requires high-level cross-cultural skills.

The most profound result of economic globalization is the integration of millions of new producers and consumers as full participants in the international economy. Twenty years ago it appeared that most of the "third world" was being relegated to the production of primary commodities for the industrial West, a role that put non-Western nations at a distinct economic disadvantage. Today, the dynamic economic growth in the Asia-Pacific region, for example, is based on enhanced technological capacity and human resource development. While economic globalization has stimulated the need for several thousand more professionals and managers with a sophisticated understanding of international trade, multicultural markets, and related cosmopolitan issues, globalization has also produced the need for hundreds of thousands of skilled workers and managers with backgrounds in finance, production, planning, and other basic business areas. There is strong demand for high-quality internationally oriented M.B.A.s and the number of such students will increase. But there is an explosion in the demand for bookkeepers, accountants, computer programmers, middle-level managers, and similarly educated workers. Millions of people around the world are making the transition from subsistence agriculture and low-skill employment to increasingly higher-skill employment.

---

[1]Paul Krugman, *Pop Internationalism* (Cambridge, Mass.: Massachusetts Institute of Technology, 1996).

Tertiary education is beginning to reflect the impact of globalization at the highest levels of professional specialization. This impact will be felt strongly in the next several years as the demand for general education and training far exceeds current mechanisms of supply. Already, rapid and sustained economic growth along the Pacific Rim is creating a demand for tertiary education that far exceeds localized supply. Moreover, while substantial national and private investments are being made to increase the delivery of tertiary education to the region, current and projected demand is well beyond the supply capacity of traditional educational delivery systems. For example, each year in Indonesia over 500,000 students complete secondary school, but only 10 percent are able to enter the tertiary education system. Similar results hold for most of the newly industrialized economies (NIEs) in the region.

As a result of a major expansion in primary and secondary education in the 1980s, by the year 2000 the number of secondary school graduates in the Asia-Pacific region will be nearly double that of 20 years earlier. At the same time, many national economies in the region are experiencing annual economic growth rates of between 6 and 8 percent. The demand for tertiary education, combined with the need for educated workers, is simply beyond the capacity of the current tertiary education system. Local providers of tertiary education generally have no excess capacity. Only a relatively small number of advantaged students are able to benefit from educational opportunities in Japan, Australia, Canada, the United States, or the European Union, where excess capacity exists. For most others, study abroad is financially impossible. A "middle-class" family in Bangkok or Jakarta or in most of that region cannot afford the living costs and full-fee tuition charged by the most affordable tertiary institution in an advanced economy. The 1.2 million-student "international market" for higher education identified by UNESCO represents only a fraction of the number of students who want higher education and who have some resources to invest in it.

Table 1 demonstrates both the burgeoning need for educated workers and the increasing ability of workers and families to pay for education. But even these figures may not fully project the potential for educational demand over the next 5 to 10 years.

The so-called "Asian Tigers" and most other rapidly expanding economies are currently experiencing the typical pattern of growth resulting from investment in economic "inputs" such as capital stock and education of workers. From a very modest base, input-led growth produces dramatic rates of increase. Eventually, however, input-led growth—to oversimplify, more people producing more stuff—must be followed by output-led growth, or actual improvement in the efficiency of production, whereby each worker produces much more per unit of input.

The transition from input-led growth to output-led growth is not automatic (the Soviet Union is a case in point), but when it happens (consider mid-nineteenth-century England or late twentieth-century Japan) the economic takeoff is precipitous.

The integrated nature of the globalized economy may encourage the successful transition from input-led to output-led growth. With cars, computers, televisions, and other products assembled from parts made in several different countries, there are powerful inducements to ensuring that production efficiencies are widely distributed.

Some suggest that the globalized economy is configuring itself for an unprecedented period of sustained growth. Stuart Kauffman has written:

Table 1
Leading Indicators of Demand for Tertiary Education in Selected Asia Pacific Economic Cooperation (APEC) Economies

	Population (millions)	Per Capita Gross Domestic Product	1995 Economic Growth	Mean Years of Schooling	Secondary Enrollment	Tertiary Enrollment
China	1,190	$2,300	10.2%	5	51%	2%
Indonesia	200	$3,150	7.1	4	38	7
Korea	45	$11,270	6.7	9	90	31
Malaysia	19	$7,930	8.2	5	58	6
Philippines	69	$2,670	6.1	8	74	38
Thailand	59	$6,260	8.2	4	33	20
Australia	17	$18,300	4.1	12	82	40
Japan	125	$20,700	1.2	11	92	32
United States	260	$25,500	3.3	12	81	66

Sources: Governments of Korea, Indonesia, Thailand; Organization for Economic Cooperation and Development; Pacific Economic Cooperation Council; World Bank.

Ambassadors of U.S. Higher Education

On a larger scale, persistent innovation in an economy may depend on its supracritical character. New goods and services create niches that call forth the innovations of further new goods and services. Each may unleash growth both because of increasing returns in the early phase of improvement on learning curves or new open markets . . . ushering out many old technologies, ushering in new ones in vast avalanches. Such avalanches create enormous areas of increasing returns because of the massive early improvements climbing learning curves along the novel technological trajectories, as well as major new markets. So such large avalanches drive significant capital formation and growth.[2]

The integrated nature of the global economy, combined with increasingly open markets and a compulsion to innovate, may be approaching the supracritical level.

But fundamental to output-led growth is knowledge and the application of knowledge, which is preeminently a function of education. Moreover, there is cause for real concern that current education systems are incapable of responding to the present—not to speak of the potential—demand for knowledge. Failure to provide the necessary educational inputs will undermine the transition to output-led growth and ultimately result in economic stagnation.

The best instructional practices, curricula, assessment processes, and validation procedures tend not to be mass-produced. Yet anyone involved in the education system knows that there is a great deal of unnecessary individual reinvention and rework. The isolation of faculty and classrooms has resulted in what is barely more than a massive cottage industry. Even guild-like elements of educational cooperation are often perceived as innovative by many educators. There is plenty of opportunity for increasing educational productivity, and an increasing need to do so.

Implications of Technological
Advances for Higher Education

The strong demand for tertiary education, combined with the innate limitations of the traditional delivery system, supports the development

---

[2]Stuart Kauffman, *At Home in the Universe* (Oxford University Press, 1995).

≋ *Further, in North America, the Asia Pacific, Central Europe, and other regions, the financial incentives and resources exist to allow an Internet-based, tertiary education system to be largely self-sustaining.*

of an alternative system. Recently, mechanisms for delivering an Internet-based tertiary education system have substantially advanced. The telecommunications infrastructure necessary for wide distribution of such an Internet-based system is quickly expanding, the cost of accessing this system is falling, and the potential educational effectiveness of the system is growing. It is now possible, where only 24 months ago it was *not* reasonably possible, to provide students with access to meaningful content and expert educational guidance on a range of topics and issues—anytime and from nearly anywhere. Over the next year, the rapid growth of the Internet is likely to result in increasing brownouts and other problems, but solutions will follow that will further enhance the reliability and accessibility of the network.

Further, in North America, the Asia Pacific, Central Europe, and other regions, the financial incentives and resources exist to allow an Internet-based, tertiary education system to be largely self-sustaining. The convergence of several recent telecommunications and computing technologies is fundamental to the practical development of a virtual means of delivering higher education. These technological advances include:

- The development of the World Wide Web (WWW) and Web browsers has substantially enhanced the ease of using the Internet. The graphic characteristics of the WWW facilitate delivery of multimedia, which support multiple approaches to teaching and learning. The WWW is an increasingly robust source of current and archival information on a very wide range of topics. Browsers, in turn, have removed much of the tedium and reduced the technological sophistication previously required to utilize the Internet to access information or to communicate. These technologies have given ordinary people access to an extraordinary on-line library and international forum for exchange of opinions and information.

- The proliferation of broadband connections enhances the user's ability to access the full potential of the WWW. This is particularly true in the Asia-Pacific region, where terrestrial fiber-optic lines are the foundational element of the telecommunications infrastructure that is currently being installed. Unlike advanced economies, where a less capable analog/copper system is already in place, many NIEs will

Ambassadors of U.S. Higher Education

leapfrog to broadband digital capacity with their first terrestrial networks. This means that use of dense media, such as real-time video-conferencing, is likely to be possible in many NIEs even before it is accessible in many advanced economies.

- By autumn 1996 a range of comparatively inexpensive Internet access devices had arrived on the market. These so-called Internet "appliances" will facilitate access to and interaction with the WWW without a full-service personal computer. Often designed to be plugged into the users' television, these devices will make access to the Internet affordable for a wide range of potential users.

Over the next five years, and beyond, each of these three techno-logical trends will continue to advance. The WWW and Web browsers will increasingly support more robust access and interaction. Forms of embedded software will allow WWW users to manipulate on-line resources in a variety of ways. Terrestrial fiber-optic networks will be sup-plemented by wireless means of accessing the Internet. Using low-cost Internet appliances to connect to the WWW via low earth orbit (LEO) satellites will put a virtual university within reach of millions of poten-tial students.

The various technologies on which the Internet depends are increas-ingly available, increasingly easy to use, and increasingly affordable. There is a readiness to pay for access to these technologies. In advanced economies, many scholars, business people, and other potential edu-cation providers are already utilizing the Internet. It provides the most appropriate means to connect those with the need and demand for tertiary education with the information resources and educational guidance that are available. As is often the case, the current problem is not so much an imbalance of supply and demand as a problem of acces-sibility to supply. For the purposes of tertiary education, in particular, the Internet can address the problem of accessibility.

A Critical Role for Quality Assurance
A few U.S. institutions have initiated strong and comprehensive inter-national operations. There are also a few examples of effective distance education programs. But given the expanding demand for tertiary

education and training, the number of such programs is very small. Why?

In part, the small number of such programs is due to limited means of delivery. The Internet-based approaches outlined above are very new and not yet fully in place. Until now, operating internationally has most often required the deployment of faculty and administrators to locations substantially unlike home campuses. International program staff often suffer from a "foreign legion" reputation: admired for their daring and deprecated for their eccentric decision to step outside the academic mainstream. It can be extremely difficult to staff and support geographically distant programs.

There are generally very few incentives for faculty or institutions to take on the extra problems (and opportunities) of international programs. Some studies have found that participation in such programs can be detrimental to a faculty member's tenure review. Most public institutions do not receive state subsidies for international programs, which have financial implications that many public institutions prefer to avoid. The start-up costs of international programs are well beyond the means of most private institutions.

Once international programs are in place, "production" of a culturally-laden service such as education, well outside its home culture, is full of truly challenging administrative, ethical, and cross-cultural issues. (Refer to Dorn's and Reafsnyder's case studies for details.)

In many cases, the preceding circumstances result in international programs that are stillborn, or at best stepchildren of the university. The programs struggle with turnovers in leadership (Dorn is a remarkable exception, having been the on-site administrator of SIUC-Niigata for nearly eight years), high faculty turnover, and a failure to maintain academic standards.

Overall, the result has generally been an ecology of failure, where prior problems justify current problems and low expectations produce the results that were expected.

All these problems and disincentives will be magnified as international programs turn to Internet-based and other technological means of educational delivery. The foreign legion reputation is likely to be fused with a "Star Trek" reputation that will hardly inspire involvement by the very best faculty and administrators. Technologically enabled vehicles for educational delivery will require new pedagogies and assessment mechanisms specifically appropriate for distance education. There is a great deal of precedence for faculty resistance to the introduction of new methods. Already, faculty and administrators, as well as institutions and statehouses, have battled over the introduction and expansion of technologically enabled education.

Despite all these impediments, the international delivery of tertiary education and training by virtual means will, over the next quarter century, become a significant element of higher education. It will overcome these substantial impediments because the cost of not doing so is too high.

The economic and social progress of dozens of nation-states and millions of people depends on expanded access to tertiary education. The growth in demand over the next quarter century will dwarf the massive expansion of higher education that the United States experienced in the 1950s and 1960s. It is not financially feasible to construct a sufficient number of brick and mortar campuses to accommodate this dramatic increase in demand. Even if it were, it is not possible to prepare enough qualified faculty to staff such traditional universities. In much of the world over the next generation, providing tertiary education and training will involve connecting widely dispersed demand to concentrations of educational supply via telecommunications systems of various types. Quality assurance mechanisms will play a critical role in this process.

Quality assurance agencies, especially those associated with ministries of education, could be very effective in discouraging and delaying the emergence of these new educational services. Mumbled concerns about the "accreditors" or the "ministry" have served to kill a great deal of innovation. In other cases, quality assurance agencies have attempted to remain neutral or even to encourage innovation, but have advocated standards inappropriate to new learning environments.

Because innovation is always risky, perhaps especially in education, it is helpful if quality assurance mechanisms minimize the risk students are expected to share. Because risk is often undertaken by those with the least to lose, quality assurance processes can establish criteria for a reasonable likelihood of student and program success. In case of failure, quality assurance processes can provide mechanisms by which students have appropriate options for continuing their study.

Because the emerging forms of education are innovative, there is a need for careful assessment and continual improvement. If the focus of quality assurance agencies is on continual improvement, they will contribute substantially to the ability of tertiary education to respond effectively to unprecedented need. In his chapter, Steven Crow states, "Excellence in international education requires a clear vision of educational objectives, a strong commitment to those charged with implementing that vision, and a sound system of evaluation. Excellence also requires that the home institution have the willingness to learn from its experiences and to strengthen as necessary its support to ensure that students abroad learn what is taught." Consistent application of this vision is in the interest of all stakeholders.

Entering the Fourth Dimension

The university, in a form vaguely recognizable, is nearly 900 years old. For most of these nine centuries, each university has existed as a specific point on a very high plane. Until the last half-century this plane had no real third dimension in terms of its extension into the population as a whole.

Following World War II, the massification of higher education in much of North America and Europe provided depth. The resulting three-dimensional university grew quickly and its shadow spread over many parts of these societies. But each university remained, as it had from its medieval origins, a point on a Euclidean plane: located in a particular place and providing instruction at particular times.

The third dimension of university education will continue to develop as the process of massification moves well beyond its Atlantic origins. But the most profound potential of the emerging era is non-Euclidean—the opportunity to transcend the limitations of space and time. Faculty in Paris or Beijing will be able to engage students in Penang or Boston. Learning will occur when it is convenient to learners. Relational data bases will record and provide access to learning and teaching, and allow these archives to be adapted for new learning experiences.

For those of us accustomed to a three-dimensional world, a fourth dimension can be difficult to envision, even disorienting. But as the university moves into the fourth dimension, it will provide greater access and opportunity for millions around the world. It must do so with a commitment to quality.

Philip J. Palin is a senior partner with The Laurasian Institution, a not-for-profit organization engaged in the design and administration of international education programs. He serves on the board of governors of the APEC Education Foundation, is a member of the Council for Quality Assurance in International Education, and was on the founding committee of the Global Alliance for Transnational Education. He can be contacted by e-mail at <ppalin@laurasian.org>

APPENDIX 1

Symposium Participants

The following people participated in the national symposium, "Does U.S. Higher Education Need a Foreign Policy?" held June 20–21, 1994, at the Chauncey Center in Princeton, New Jersey, and/or in the December 12, 1994 meeting held in Washington, D.C., at which the *Standards for Evaluating Credit-Bearing Programs Abroad* were drafted:

Carin Berg—European Centre for Higher Education: United Nations Educational, Cultural, and Scientific Organization (UNESCO)

Richard Brecht—National Foreign Language Center

Barbara Burn—University of Massachusetts/Amherst and the Association of International Education Administrators

Naomi Collins—NAFSA: Association of International Educators

Steven D. Crow—Commission on Institutions of Higher Education, North Central Association of Colleges and Schools

John Deupree—The College Board

Richard Dye—Institute of International Education

Sherril Gelmon—Association of Specialized and Professional Accreditors

Dale Gough—American Association of Collegiate Registrars and Admissions Officers

Mary Ann Hennessey—The Council of Europe

Marjorie Peace Lenn—Center for Quality Assurance in International Education

David Maxwell—National Foreign Language Center

Philip Palin—The Laurasian Institution

William Paver—University of Texas at Austin and the American Association of Collegiate Registrars and Admissions Officers

Charles Reafsnyder—Indiana University

Billie Stewart—National Policy Board on Higher Education Institutional Accreditation

David Stewart—American Council on Education

Donald M. Stewart—The College Board

Barbara Turlington—American Council on Education

The National Symposium was made possible through a grant from the TOEFL Policy Council. Representing the Educational Testing Service at the symposium: Nancy Cole, Robert L. Albright, Jeannette File-Lamb, Jacqueline Ross, and Russell Webster.

Ambassadors of U.S. Higher Education

APPENDIX 2

Reference Sources for International Educational Program Standards

California State University Systems Office. 1988. *Executive Order on State-Funded Campus Study Abroad Programs in the California State University*. Long Beach, Calif.

Commission on Higher Education, Middle States Association of Colleges and Schools. 1993. *Report of the Task Force on Accreditation Issues in International Education*. Philadelphia, Pa.

Council on Postsecondary Accreditation, Regional Institutional Accrediting Bodies. 1990. *Principles of Good Practice in Overseas International Education Programs for Non-U.S. Nationals*. Washington, D.C.

Council on Standards for International Educational Travel. 1991. *Advisory List of International Educational Travel and Exchange Programs*. Washington, D.C.

Greene, William A., Broward Community College, and the International/Intercultural Consortium of the American Association of Community and Junior Colleges. 1988. *Developing American Two-Year College Programs Abroad*. Florida and Washington, D.C.

International Education Forum. 1991. *Journal of the Association of International Education Administrators*. Athens, Ohio: Ohio University.

National Association for Foreign Student Affairs. 1983. *NAFSA Principles for International Educational Exchange*. Washington, D.C.

North Central Association of Colleges and Schools. 1988. *Issues in International Education*. NCA Quarterly. Chicago, Ill.

North Central Association of Colleges and Schools. 1988. *A Practical Guide for Organizing and Conducting International Evaluation Visits*. Chicago, Ill.

North Central Association of Colleges and Schools. 1989. *Site Visits at Overseas Programs*. Chicago, Ill.